Harry Redknapp

Harry Redknapp

MY AUTOBIOGRAPHY

with Derek McGovern

CollinsWillow

An Imprint of HarperCollins*Publishers*

First published in 1998
by CollinsWillow
an imprint of HarperCollins*Publishers*
London

© Harry Redknapp 1998

1 3 5 7 9 8 6 4 2

A CIP catalogue record for this book is
available from the British Library

ISBN 0 00 218872 4

Printed and bound in Great Britain by
Caledonian International Book Manufacturing Ltd, Glasgow

All photographs supplied by Harry Redknapp
with the exception of the following:
Action Images picture no. 5, 26, 36, 38; **Allsport** 24, 35, 39;
Associated Press 40; **Colorsport** 4; **Alan Cozzi** 22, 32, 41;
Empics 7, 27; **Trevor Jones** 23; **Mirror Syndication International** 21, 37, 42;
PA News 19, 28; **Popperfoto** 9, 25; **Rex Features** 12, 18;
Southern Newspapers Plc 30, 31; **Sporting Pictures (UK) Ltd** 8, 33, 34

Contents

Foreword
by Jamie Redknapp

Harry Redknapp is my Dad – he's also my idol.

I wouldn't have been a footballer had it not been for my Dad's constant encouragement and sound advice. He was never one to stand on the touchline shouting and screaming like other fathers of promising young players. But I know that whenever I have something troubling me, football-related or not, I can rely on Dad to help me out. I ring him virtually every day and return to my parents' home in Bournemouth whenever I can.

I remember as a kid Dad used to take me training at Bournemouth when I should have been behind my desk at school. My Mum would have gone crazy had she known, but Dad always made sure when he took me home at 4pm that I was wearing my school uniform. He just knew that I was going to be a footballer and believed an education on the training ground would benefit me more than a double lesson of logarithms. And he was right. Those days kicking a ball around during training with Bournemouth helped me to grow up quickly. I was around adults, adult humour, adult conversation – and I was a quick learner.

As a manager Dad wears his heart on his sleeve. He's incredibly passionate about the game, and though he has this laugh-a-minute, devil-may-care image, I know he's a worrier. Some managers don't seem to be affected by bad results but you can see Dad hurting. He worries about doing his job well, about what people think.

I think Dad is very well liked inside football. As a coach he's second to none. I've been fortunate to work with some top-class coaches and Dad's right up there with the best of them. He brings a sense of fun to his workplace. He brings enthusiasm, and he's full of ideas. Players like Dad and respect him.

One of the worst moments of my life was going to see Dad in Italy after the horrific car crash which killed his best mate Brian Tiler. Brian was a great bloke and we were all heartbroken. We got to the hospital at 11pm and at first they wouldn't let us in to see Dad. That made us worry even more. I remember vividly walking into a ward with 10 beds and Dad's was in the far corner. He was facing the wall and as I called his name I was unprepared for the shock I was about to suffer. He turned slowly to face us – and was unrecognizable. Ghostly white, scars all over his face, he looked near death. I'm not too proud to admit that this grown-up 15-year-old kid fainted. I woke up with a wet towel around my head being attended to by a nurse. What an egg. Dad, despite his horrific injuries, was more worried about me.

Dad has been the perfect tutor to me – both on the pitch and off. He says in this book that I make him proud. Really it's the other way round. He's my confidante, my counsel, my mate, my idol. Above all he's my Dad. And that makes me proudest of all.

Introduction

As I enter my fifth year as West Ham manager I would need only one wish for all my dreams to come true. There is no one prouder of this job than me but with such pride comes a sense of sorrow, sorrow that two of my greatest friends are no longer around to share my good fortune.

Bobby Moore was not only my dear friend, he was also my staunchest ally. I remember listening to the radio on the way to a match the day after John Lyall's departure as West Ham manager and Bobby was asked who would be the ideal replacement.

'There's only one man for the job,' he said. 'Harry Redknapp.'

I can't tell you what a lift that gave me. The thought that a man of Bobby's stature, a legend of the game, was so strongly in my court was strangely touching. How cruel that his life was cut so tragically short by cancer.

Brian Tiler was a massive influence on me during my early

days in management at Bournemouth. Brian was a constant source of encouragement through good times and bad. Whenever my confidence dwindled it was Brian who bucked me up. He was convinced that I would succeed at the very highest levels of the game and the car crash that claimed his life robbed me of another very dear friend. It's my one wish that those two could stand at my shoulder today, to see that their faith in me was justified.

I'm sure if Bobby and Brian are looking down on me now, they'll raise a glass to the memories I share in this book. They were part of so many.

It's my good luck that I can share my day-to-day life as a Premiership manager with Frank Lampard – my brother-in-law, my closest friend, and my right-hand man at Upton Park. I know Bobby would be proud because he thought the world of Frank.

They say you can choose your friends but you can't choose your family. In that case it's lucky for me that I've been blessed with the best. I dedicate this book to my lovely wife Sandra, to my two sons Mark and Jamie, and to my Mum and Dad. They've all stood behind me during the bad times; now I want them to share in the good. And for them all I've got one simple message. Thanks.

Harry Redknapp

CHAPTER 1

Bonds of Friendship

Y ou don't reach the half-century mark in life without harbouring some regrets. One of my biggest is the break-up of my friendship with my best mate Billy Bonds, an all-time favourite at Upton Park. I was best man at Bill's wedding – now we haven't spoken for four years. That's a serious breakdown – one I will attempt to explain as honestly and as fully as I can.

I know that many West Ham fans still wonder about the background to my replacing Bill as Hammers manager on the eve of the 1994–95 season. 'Did Harry stab his best pal in the back?' is the gist of their thoughts. I know in my heart of hearts, and I sincerely hope Bill feels the same, that nothing could be further from the truth. But before quoting chapter and verse on those controversial days before I was appointed West Ham's boss, it is necessary to go back to the early Sixties, when I was a raw teenager, to chart the beginning of what on paper seemed an unlikely friendship.

Bill and I first met at Lilleshall during a week-long series of trials for the England youth side. Bill was at Charlton at the time; I was at West Ham. I managed to impress the selectors a little more than Bill and made it into the side which went on to win the Junior World Cup in Holland, in 1964.

Looking back it was no surprise that we did so well because the team was packed with talent. Peter Springett was in goal, with Mickey Wright, who went on to play for years with Aston Villa, the right-back. A boy called Bobby Noble was left-back and what a player he was. He would have gone on to win many full international caps but suffered a serious car crash when he was 21 while with Manchester United and didn't play again. A sad loss to the game. Bobby was magnificent. Off the field he was every inch the teddy boy from the Moss Side area of Manchester; on it he was the ultimate professional. Alfie Woods, of Manchester City was also at the back. Then how about this for a midfield: Howard Kendall, John Hollins, John Sissons and Peter Knowles. Up front there was David Sadler, who went on to represent Manchester United so wonderfully, Don Rogers, who many will remember scaring the life out of Arsenal in the 1969 League Cup Final for Swindon, and yours truly. To give you an idea of how far ahead of every other nation's youth squad we were, we played Spain in the World Cup Final and absolutely murdered them 4–0. We were different class.

Those trials were my first meeting with Bill, but we did not become mates until much later when he was signed by West Ham for £47,500, which was a lot of money in those days. Right from the start we hit it off which, given our respective make-ups, is something of a surprise. I'm known as a chirpy, garrulous kind of guy but Bill in stark contrast is a complete non-mixer. In fact some might even say he's almost anti-social, but he had his family and that was enough for him. In all the time he was at West Ham, he never went into the players' bar after a game. He'd get to the ground, play the game, and by 5 o'clock on a Saturday he'd be bombing away from Upton

Park, hair soaking wet, shirt undone, through the Blackwall Tunnel and home. He never mixed with anyone socially at all. I used to give him stick over it but it didn't seem to bother him. It was just his way.

We'd been big mates for several years by the time of my wedding to my wife, Sandra, in June 1968, and naturally I wanted him to be part of the big day. Yet a few hours before the ceremony he phoned and told me that he wouldn't be able to come because his auntie was sick. I slagged him off unmercifully and eventually forced him to turn up, although I don't think he wanted to be there. But that's what he was like. Looking back, perhaps this was a punishment for my performance at his wedding. Bill had asked me to be best man but I think he regrets that to this day. I ruined all the pictures, he said, because I had my hands in my pockets in every one. I also got him into trouble with his in-laws when I read out the telegrams, pretending they were from William Hills and Ladbrokes! If looks could kill...

We were room-mates at West Ham and used to spend our Friday nights before a game at the dog track. I know in this day and age that sounds remarkable but that's the way things were then. In fact me and Bill got involved in owning a greyhound but that wasn't a happy experience. It was called Outcast Hunter and first time out it finished fifth of six. Its next race was at Slough so Billy and I went to the track to watch our little investment perform with a view to having a decent bet. But the trainer told us it had no chance. It was just having a run to keep fit. Outcast Hunter opened up at 5–1 and was promptly backed off the boards. By the time we realized what was going on it was too late to get a bet on, the hare was already running. Needless to say, it won. We'd been had over by the trainer which was a real liberty. We took Outcast Hunter away from the trainer to run at West Ham dogs but it never won again. Bill ended up taking it home as a pet.

I must have spent five years with Bill at West Ham and what

a player he was. He was unique, a one-off. You read nowadays of all these new-fangled pasta diets which are supposed to be the only things footballers can eat, but Bill used to wolf down a big plate of steak and kidney pie, chips and peas with about eight slices of bread and butter at noon on a match day and still get through twice as much work in a game as anyone else. No wonder the punters loved him.

After his playing career had ended in 1986, Bill stayed on at Upton Park as youth team coach, with John Lyall the manager. John was later replaced by Lou Macari, who didn't last long, but before Lou got the job I had been approached by West Ham. I was manager at Bournemouth at the time, around June 1989, and things had gone really well for me. Martin Cearns, then West Ham chairman and today still a director at the club, told me the Hammers had received several applications for the manager's job but mine was not among them. He asked if I'd be interested.

'Yeah, of course I would be,' I said.

'Terrific,' he said. 'We'll meet up and have a chat. If things go well you've got the job.'

Unfortunately things are not as straightforward as that in football. A warning bell should have sounded when he then asked: 'Should I speak to your chairman or do you think you should have a word first?' I was as naive as he was and didn't really know how to go about these things so I said the best bet was for me to speak to my chairman, a lovely guy called Jim Nolan who I got on really well with. I told Brian Tiler, then managing director at Bournemouth and also my best mate, about West Ham's interest and he didn't sound surprised. 'It was only a matter of time,' he said. 'You've done well here, bigger clubs were bound to come sniffing. Let's go and have a word with the chairman.'

But Nolan was having none of it. He was furious at what he saw as an illegal approach by West Ham and phoned Martin Cearns, threatening to report West Ham to the League. Under those circumstances I could have walked out on Bournemouth and let the two clubs sort out all the argy-bargy between them. But how could I do that? Bournemouth had treated me so well and my home was in the town so I decided not to force the issue. I think at the same time West Ham got cold feet about the illegal approach threat and everything blew over. The next minute Lou Macari was appointed. I suppose you could say I was a little disappointed at being robbed of the opportunity of managing a bigger club but I was happy at Bournemouth and, remember, it was West Ham who came chasing me, not the other way round. Anyway, Macari did not have the happiest of times at Upton Park and was replaced within eight months by my mate Bill.

When Hammers were relegated a couple of seasons later Bill gave me a call. I immediately thought something must be up because Bill never phoned *anyone*. As it turned out, he was a bit unhappy with the way things were going and told me he could do with a bit of help. By this stage things had changed at Bournemouth. I'd been involved in a horrific car accident in Italy in 1990 that tragically claimed the life of my good pal Brian Tiler, and when I returned to the club after my convalescence there was a new chairman, Ken Gardiner, in control. And just before Bill made his offer I'd decided the time was right to leave Bournemouth after a run-in with Gardiner. Grabbing your chairman by the throat is not the best career move for a manager, you'd have to say. But shrewdly mapping out a career has never been my strong suit. Gardiner deserved a reprimand for what I saw was a disgusting remark he made about Brian Tiler.

We had just played Reading at home in the last game of the 1991–92 season and were in the vice-president's lounge with all the club officials and a group of supporters – all mates of mine, local people I'd known for years – who had paid a few quid extra to be entertained following the final whistle. I'd have hoped they'd have been entertained *before* the final whistle, too, but that wasn't always the case. The chairman was making a presentation to the barman, who was leaving after 19 years of service. There was Ken, an old Bournemouthian, very posh, pipe in mouth, banging the gavel in that High Court judge sort of way to appeal for order. At that moment, my centre half Kevin Bond walked in straight from the dressing room, gasping for a drink, and thirstily, possibly even noisily, ordered a lager. Ken banged down his gavel even harder and boomed: 'Can I have some silence – and that includes you, Kevin Bond,' in the way a schoolteacher would address his pupils. To be honest it was very embarrassing, not just for Kevin but for everyone in the room. Kevin put down his drink and walked out.

'What was all that about?' I said to Ken after the presentation was over.

'Well,' he said, 'I did not wish to be interrupted when I was making a presentation to a man who's given 19 years of service to this club.'

I made a flippant remark to which Ken took exception, and he reacted by casting a slur on the good name of Brian Tiler. It was a nasty remark, still difficult to forgive even after all these years, and it infuriated me. I got him by the throat, in front of about 150 people, and God knows what I'd have done had someone not dragged me off him. He was the chairman. It wasn't quite the thing to do. Ken demanded an apology but there was more chance of me swimming the ocean. *He* wanted an apology? *I* wanted the apology. And that was it. Time to move on.

When Bill rang that summer and started talking about someone helping him at West Ham I thought I wouldn't mind some of that. In truth I'd had enough of managing. I'd had nine years at Bournemouth and that was plenty. I enjoyed coaching and I thought I could earn a nice little living at Upton Park, getting out with the players without the worries and stresses that go hand in hand with being a full-time boss. That's how I saw it going. After nine years of doing everything – coaching, out every night scouting, picking teams – I just thought it was time for a change.

I was appointed assistant boss of West Ham in July 1992 and what I first saw at Upton Park shook me to the core. It was frightening. The club was going absolutely nowhere. They'd just been relegated with one of the lowest points totals in history and the highlight of the season was beating Manchester United in the match that robbed Alex Ferguson's men of the title. That's the game, if you remember, that really gave Fergie the needle. He called West Ham's performance 'obscene' and in a way you can perhaps understand him. After all, if they were capable of turning in a display like that once they'd already been relegated, how come they couldn't manage it more often during the season when survival was still a very real prospect?

I was happy to work alongside Bill. He deserved success for everything he'd put into the club, but morale was at a low ebb and I remember thinking from the first minute I arrived 'this is going to be tough'. Things were bad. A few players in the squad just didn't care and the general confidence level was zero. When it came to our first pre-season home game the players were too frightened to go out for a kickabout before the game. I told them to go out on the pitch and loosen up but they just made excuses. They remembered all too vividly the stick they had taken from the fans the previous season.

In our first game we won at Barnsley 1–0 thanks to a Clive Allen goal – a good start but it served only to paper over the very wide cracks. Following a defeat at Charlton, we went to Newcastle in the third match and got well turned over in a 2–0 defeat. Yet within five minutes of getting on the coach home from St James' Park the lagers were out and the players were laughing and joking. Loyal West Ham punters had paid good money to travel all the way to the north-east to watch this lot, yet there was a mob at the back who were clearly not bothered by an embarrassing defeat.

I knew right away serious changes had to be made for the good of the club, dead wood had to be shifted. I think if Bill was honest he'd say he didn't have a lot of time for the players. He'd been such a good player himself, a whole-hearted servant of the club, and I think deep down the thought of some of them earning high-grade salaries for low-grade performances disgusted him. That attitude was understandable, but it didn't help when you had to get players to turn it on for you. I saw it as one of my first tasks to lift the players, to instil confidence, to tell them constantly how good they were. At the same time stricter discipline was essential. There's no doubt that one or two of them had been on the booze and let themselves go. I decided we had to train them harder, and get them to lose a bit of weight.

One morning our centre half Colin Foster rang in and left a message with the physio that he couldn't come training. When I asked why, I was told the contract with the club's sponsors had expired and they'd taken back their courtesy cars. Consequently Foster couldn't get in for training. Can you believe it? This was a professional football club yet the players were acting like Sunday League performers. So we rang Foster at home only to get his answerphone. No doubt he was out shopping with his missus. When I confronted him about it the next day he just didn't seem able to accept that he could have caught a bus or taxi, that he was on thousands of pounds a week for doing something half the country would do for nothing. His wife had to use the other car to get to work, he said, so he was stranded. 'This ain't real', I thought. That's a symptom of how the club was. I'm not saying it was all the players – many of them were as good as gold – but the poison of the rotten apples was beginning to spread.

I suppose in a way I was a bit of a disappointment to the players when I first arrived. Not from a professional point of view I hasten to add. It was just that they'd been led to believe that Harry Redknapp was this laugh-a-minute guy who was going to cheer everyone up but when I got to Upton Park there was nothing to laugh about. After that Newcastle defeat we had a no-holds-barred clear-the-air meeting when a few strong opinions were expressed. Our centre half Tony Gale, a good pro, said something which probably changed me as much as I changed the players.

'We'd heard that you were coming and that you were bright and chirpy but you've been a miserable bastard. You haven't stopped moaning since you've been here,' he said.

I thought: 'Fair enough, he's right.' I could feel myself weighed down by the dourness of it all. It was all gloom and doom. No spark. I was growling and groaning all the time and that was probably the last thing we needed. Bill was a quieter character than me and to complement him I needed to be my normal self, to have a laugh and a joke and keep things bubbly. I tried to get in among the lads and get to know them and maybe that was one of the things that helped improve the club's fortunes.

My experience of managing in the lower leagues had taught me which players could do a job if stepped up in class. I bought a boy called Peter Butler, a really good midfield competitor, from Southend, and Mark Robson on a free from Spurs and they turned out to be terrific signings.

Things began steadily to improve. My partnership with Bill was great. We got on so well, no problems whatsoever. He was the gaffer but he let me get on with training and after the first couple of months I really enjoyed the coaching aspect without the aggravation of being manager. As morale rose so too did our position in the table, so much so that towards the end of the season we looked a certainty for automatic promotion alongside Newcastle. But then Portsmouth put together a fantastic late run of something like 10 consecutive wins and suddenly they were three points above us with two games each left to go. They went to Sunderland on the Saturday and got beat 4–1; the following day we won 3–1 at

Swindon, a perfect set of results that put us level on points with Pompey but with a better goal difference because of that massive turnaround in the space of 24 hours. From being dead and buried we were right back in it. On the final day we had to beat Cambridge at home by a bigger margin than Portsmouth beat Grimsby. An added worry was that Cambridge had to win to stay up and their manager Ian Atkins had pinned on the dressing-room wall a comment made by West Ham's Ian Bishop that 'Cambridge ought to be a formality.' On a day of unbelievable tension we ended up winning 2–0 with goals from David Speedie, and Clive Allen in the very last minute. Portsmouth could only win 2–1 and we were back in the top flight.

Against all the odds – the bookies had made us favourites to go straight down again – we did okay in the Premiership the following season, despite losing our first two games at home to Wimbledon and away to Leeds. We improved the squad again without spending any real money. The big change was the sale a month into the season of Hammers cult hero Julian Dicks to Liverpool. I'll explain the thinking behind that move later. It was one that could have got both Bill and I the sack but in fact worked in our favour. We'd struggled up to then but Dicksy's departure was the turning point and in a season of consolidation we were delighted to finish 13th.

I was the instigator of the Dicks transfer so I suppose observers may have suspected at that time that I was taking on an increasingly high-profile role, but wheeling and dealing was what I was good at and Bill let me get on with it. He was very laid-back in that respect and gave me all the rope in the world. Bill was still up front as the manager but he was happy to let me have my say. Looking back, that first season back in the Premiership was very much the calm before the storm. Our relationship at that time was different class. We never had an argument, never a hint of an angry exchange. In fact, if two men were ever born to work as a team, it was Bill and I. It was against this background that the events at the start of the 1994–95 season were so hard to stomach.

In truth the first seeds were sown during our pre-season tour to Scotland, at a time when my old club Bournemouth were up for sale. While in Scotland I received a call from Geoffrey Hayward, a former chairman at Dean Court, who told me he wanted to buy the club on one condition – that I went back there.

'If you come back, Harry, I'll give you the club,' he said. 'Whatever you want, it's yours. You can be managing director, manager, whatever. Just ask.'

I must admit it was a hugely tempting offer. Okay it would have been a backward step leaving a Premiership club, but my home was still Bournemouth. That's where my wife Sandra was, my son Mark too, and it was where younger son Jamie still called home even though by now he was doing so well at Liverpool. I'm from the East End of London – Poplar to be exact, just a stone's throw from Upton Park – but Bournemouth is my home and has been for some time. I'm very popular there. Some people have said, probably jokingly, that before long I'll be Lord Mayor. I thought to myself: 'Well Harry, you're pushing 50, why not settle for an easier life?' To be honest I was very interested in Hayward's proposition. Things had gone well at West Ham. I'd helped Bill turn things around and I could leave with my head held high.

When I told Bill about the offer during our pre-season trip in Scotland, his attitude was: 'I don't blame you, Harry, it's your home. But I don't know what I'll do without you.' Then, after a pause, he said without warning: 'If you go, I'll go.' I couldn't understand it.

'Don't be stupid, Bill. What do you want to do that for?'

'Ahh, I don't want to do it any more', he said.

I told him that if he was taking that attitude then I was staying put. I certainly didn't want to be responsible for Billy walking out on his beloved West Ham. 'No,' he said. 'You do what you want to do. I may not go. We'll see what happens.'

The following day it became clear that news of Bournemouth's offer to me was about to be reported in the newspapers. Somehow news had got out from our end. I told Bill and he said we'd better go and see the chairman, Terry Brown, who was also up in Scotland with Peter Storrie, the managing director. Before long Bill, myself, the chairman and Peter Storrie were gathered in the chairman's hotel room.

'Why are you leaving?' the chairman asked me, but before I could answer he said:

'You want to be a manager, don't you?'

As much as I denied it, as much as I stressed I was itching to get back home to Bournemouth, he grilled me about my managerial ambitions. Then, out of the blue he said: 'What happens if we make you manager?'

I looked at him, aghast. 'But you've got a manager. Bill's the manager. I don't want to be manager.'

'What if we make Bill the director of football?' he replied.

'That's not the issue,' I said. 'I don't want to be manager and Bill probably doesn't want to be director of football. My only options are to carry on as before or to leave and return to Bournemouth. They're going to pay me what I'm earning here – and it's home.'

This whole conversation was being conducted in Bill's presence, and it wasn't long before he had his say. 'It's quite obvious you want Harry to take over from me,' he said. 'I'm not stupid. You think he's better at it than me. You want Harry as manager.' Things were getting very uncomfortable. This wasn't what I expected when I mentioned the offer from Bournemouth. In fact it was the last thing I wanted.

'Look Bill, hang on,' I began, but he carried on, his pride understandably damaged.

'Well what does this director of football business mean?' he asked.

The chairman outlined the functions of the job, which were

pretty flexible. He could come in for training when he liked. Turn up on match days and generally act the ambassador for the club everyone knew he already was. Crucially, he added: 'And the job's for life...'

This checked Bill for a moment, the thought of earning good money until he was 65 for doing very little obviously seeming to appeal. Bill asked for some time to think things over and confided in me that he was in two minds what to do. I could well understand. What the chairman was offering would have appealed to me too. No aggravation. A job for life. I thought to myself: 'I could do that. Coming in on a Saturday for the match and knocking back a few gin and tonics in the boardroom. I'd like some of that.' I told Bill that I genuinely did not want the West Ham manager's job. Maybe I was lacking in ambition or something, but I just didn't feel comfortable with the thought of all the aggravation. And of course there were two other factors playing on my mind; first, the tempting offer from Bournemouth; second, the growing realization that if I was to take over from Bill in the circumstances I've just described, it wouldn't take mischief-makers too long to put two and two together and make five.

I should point out here that, amid all this uncertainty, Bill and I also had to deal with the ludicrous problem of Joey Beauchamp, which I'll mention in detail later, who signed for us from Oxford for £1million and the very next day started whingeing that he'd made a mistake and wanted to go home. I think this was all getting on top of Bill, and matters had still not been resolved by the time we left Scotland and played Portsmouth in a pre-season friendly. Beauchamp turned up late for the Pompey game, made no effort on the pitch, we played poorly, and all in all it was a bad day. It was the final straw for Bill. On the Monday he phoned me.

'I'm at the ground,' he said.

'What are you doing there?' I asked.

'I'm meeting the chairman. I'm packing up.'

I jumped in the car and raced to the ground with Ronnie Boyce, another former West Ham player, to try to persuade him not to go. We arrived just in time, but try as we might we couldn't get Bill to change his mind and in he went to see the chairman. When he finally emerged the chairman asked to see me.

'Bill's going,' he said without preamble. 'Will you be the manager?'

Before I could answer he started talking about how the season was almost upon us, how he'd organized a press conference, how everything was set for me to take charge. Events were fast overtaking me. Things were becoming a blur. I managed to get hold of Bill again and told him of the chairman's offer. 'Take it, Harry, you'd be a fool not to,' he said. 'It's a good job. It's well paid. Take it.'

'But Bill, what about…' I began.

'Don't worry about me,' he said. 'I've had it off. I've been well looked after.'

With that I was almost bundled into a press conference announcing me as the new manager. Yet it wasn't something I'd wanted to happen. I allowed myself to be pushed into it too quickly and that was a mistake. That night I went home to Bournemouth having told the chairman that I was far from certain I wanted the job. I was deeply troubled, so deeply that I stayed the entire week in Bournemouth. The next morning I picked up a paper and read a story that I'd knifed Bill in the back. But that's not my game, not my nature. I would never do anything like that. I am not ambitious enough to jeopardize a friendship for the sake of a job, and certainly not to Bill of all people.

All that week I was getting calls from the club. Peter Storrie came to see me to tell me how important it was that I took the job. I phoned Bill and told him that I'd decided not to take it but he was adamant that I should say yes. 'Look Bill,' I said, broaching one of the things that was really worrying me. 'If I take this job it'll look like I've done a bad'un on you, like I've stitched you up.'

'Don't worry,' he said. 'You and I both know you haven't. Take it.'

I still wasn't convinced, but then players like Alvin Martin and Ludo Miklosko came to see me and told me they wanted me to stay. They were pleased with the way things had gone over the previous two years and said it was important I stayed. Frank Lampard, the old West Ham star who is married to my wife's sister, gave me some home truths. If you don't take the manager's job someone else will take it, he said. Bill's packed in. He's got paid up. Someone's got to have his job, so why not you?

So I took it, with Bill's blessing. But I felt our relationship started to go downhill from then on. I'm not sure it had that much to do with my decision to replace him. I think it was perhaps more to do with what followed. In football, as with other jobs, when you leave a club, people come and tell you what your successor has said, and I suppose it gets to you. It happened to me when I left Bournemouth. I recommended my assistant Tony Pulis for the manager's job, but all of a sudden he sacked the other two lads who had worked with us, Stuart Morgan and Terry Shanahan, and they were big mates of mine. These things happen. Maybe Bill in the same way was getting things fed back to him by someone who was trying to stir up trouble.

In the early days after his departure I rang him for a chat on a few occasions but looking back it must have been very hard for him. He'd fallen out with the chairman and fallen out big time with Peter Storrie and under those circumstances, I don't care who you are, you're not going to want the club to be winning every week. It's human nature. So it was fraught with difficulties. I wanted to win for my life, but Bill, still feeling bitterness, had an altogether different agenda and so we just drifted apart. But I still love him to bits.

I don't know if Bill bears me any ill-will. It bothers me more than anything to think that he might. Of all the people in football I've met, he'd be right up there at the top. I would never have done anything to harm him. I'd rather not have the job than anyone think that. I know things didn't go too well for Bill at Millwall but if he's reading this I'd like to tell him that I'd have him back at West Ham tomorrow. I'd find him a job without a moment's hesitation.

But I know Bill.

He won't ask.

CHAPTER 2

Win or Lose –
on the Booze

West Ham was a fantastic place to be in the 1960s. There was a great set of lads at the club, and we could all bask in the reflected glory of Bobby Moore, Geoff Hurst and Martin Peters, the Hammers trio who played such a key role in England's 1966 World Cup triumph.

Mooro was a God, there are no two ways about it. When I broke into the first team in the early Sixties after a golden youth career Bobby was top man at Upton Park. Everybody looked up to him. You'd have thought given his stature that he would be aloof with new kids coming into the side but from day one he looked after me. He took me under his wing and really made sure I was okay. We got on great, but he treated everyone the same way. Bobby was also a natural-born leader. When he did something, everybody followed suit. He had a superstition of putting his shorts on last before running out onto the pitch. The next minute everyone was trying to do the same. Bobby would wear a key-ring hanging out of his belt. Sure enough the rest of the players slavishly followed the trend. He was the person everybody looked up to. And he was impossible to dislike.

It amuses me nowadays to hear football fans in, say, Liverpool or Manchester, likening Mooro to royalty. I suppose to them he must have given the impression of being somewhat aloof the way he carried himself, the way he always behaved with such dignity. But, make no mistake, Mooro was one of the lads. I suppose he must have given the same impression to fans in the north that Alan Hansen did to fans in the south when he was in his prime at Liverpool. Both players were exceptionally composed, unruffled, never got their shorts dirty. Opposing players all wanted to get stuck into Bobby, to rough him up, and to shatter his immense calm.

I remember one time we were playing Hereford in the fourth round of the 1972 FA Cup and they had a player up front called Billy Meadows, who liked to get stuck in. In the previous round Hereford had knocked out Newcastle in one of the biggest Cup upsets in history, with Ron Radford scoring that spectacular winning goal. Right from the start Meadows tried to wind Mooro up, giving him the verbals about everything under the sun. Absolutely diabolical remarks. To be honest he drove Mooro mad but Bobby didn't bite. The tie ended in a 0–0 draw. It just so happened that for the replay Hereford were in the same hotel that we always used for our pre-match meal. Meadows had more front than anyone I've ever met, and right away he walked up to Bobby's table.

'All right, Mooro?' he said. 'Sorry about all that last week. I was out of order.' Bobby didn't want to know, and just nodded at him. But within minutes of the kick-off in the replay Meadows was doing exactly the same thing. Again Bobby didn't bite, but I don't think I ever saw a more determined performance from him. Meadows hardly got a kick and we won comfortably. But that's the kind of thing he had to put up with regularly.

What a player he was though. I will always remember his

performance against Pele and Brazil in the 1970 World Cup in Mexico. Before the game, Bobby had been falsely accused of stealing a bracelet from a jewellery shop in Bogota, but he put it all behind him and went out to play the game of his life against perhaps the greatest football team ever to set foot on a pitch. That Bogota business was unbelievable. Of all the people I've ever met Bobby would have been the last person to get mixed up in something like that. You could have walked into West Ham any day of the week with a £300 suit or a £500 watch and offer it to Bobby for a fiver, but he wouldn't have touched it if he thought it was in any way crooked. Everything about him was right and proper. He loved a drink, was great company to go out with, and really was one of the lads, but he would never consider anything hookey. So when he got accused of stealing that bracelet I knew it was a stitch-up. The shop assistant had allegedly stolen the bracelet and given it to her boyfriend, and then decided to pin the blame on a tourist. She picked on Bobby, without realizing who he was.

We certainly had our share of fun moments off the pitch. I remember one Christmas Eve some of the lads were in a pub called The Globe in London's East End. It was just after lunch time and the pub was packed with all the girls from the local factory having a jolly-up, and me, Bobby and a few of the lads were having a good laugh. Some time during the afternoon, the phone rang, and it was Tina, Bobby's wife, telling him they were due to go to a do that night in the West End and that he'd better get his skates on. But Bobby, far from getting his skates on, had a few more drinks. A couple of hours later the phone went again. It was Tina, by now sounding more than a little cheesed off.

'Are you coming home?'

'Yeah,' Bobby said, 'I'll be there in an hour.'

Two hours later the phone went again. Tina. 'If you don't get home right now, I'm telling your mother.'

'Yeah, okay,' Bobby said. 'I'm leaving now.'

An hour later the pub door opened and in walked Bobby's mum. The rest of us couldn't believe it. He was the captain of England, and here was his mum collecting him from the pub like a naughty schoolboy.

'Come along, Bobby,' she said, as Bobby, by now the worse for wear, stumbled to his feet. As she grabbed him by the arm she looked at the rest of us and said: 'Someone's mixed his drink.' As Mooro walked out of the pub, he must have seen the funny side of it and started laughing. 'But mum,' he said, in mock protest, 'I'm 29.' The captain of England went out like a lamb with his mum. But you knew all along that Bobby would get home in time to take Tina to the do. He just loved a drink with the lads first.

I remember another time while we were in America together, in the late Seventies, Bobby arranged for a few of us to go to see Diana Ross in her first solo concert since leaving the Supremes. We were in a hotel bar in New York having a few beers before going on to the concert and Bobby had told the barman to put everything on the tab. Before we knew it the world and his wife were putting drinks on our tab. After a couple of hours I was standing there chatting away, when a couple of bouncers lumbered up and handed me the bill – for about $1,000. Given that I had about 30 quid on me there was no way I was going to be paying, but when I looked around for the lads they'd all vanished. 'Sorry mate,' I said to them, 'they've all gone.'

'But you've got the bill,' one of them said. 'So waddya gonna do?'

I didn't have a clue what to do. Then I realized that the rest of them had probably gone ahead to the Waldorf Astoria, where Diana Ross was performing. I managed to get hold of Bobby on the phone and told him I was still at the hotel bar.

'What are you doing there?'

'I'll tell you what I'm doing here. I'm stuck here with this f****** bill.'

Bobby said: 'Well everyone else was drinking a lot more than we were so I left the bill to them.'

'That's great,' I said, 'but now I'm here on my own with the bill and there are a couple of big gorillas here not very happy with me.'

Five minutes later Bobby arrived at the bar, and paid the bill without a murmur.

Bobby had a reputation for liking the booze but he was as dedicated as any professional could ever be. However much he had to drink on a Saturday night, Bobby would turn up for training on his own on a Sunday morning to get the drink out of his system. He never missed a Sunday morning session. And he was so punctual. But the drink almost cost him his life one night. A few of the lads went down to Margate to play for Jimmy Tarbuck's XI. Tarby, who was doing a summer season there, had people like Tommy Steele and Kenny Lynch playing in the side, but we were up against most of the Margate lads, semi-pros, so it wasn't easy. After the game, we had a great jolly-up and Bobby was really in no condition to drive home. He had a great capacity for booze and must have thought he'd be okay, but he drove straight over a roundabout in his red Jag and the car was a write-off. Don't ask me how Bobby escaped unscathed but there was hardly a scratch on him.

I think his tidiness was legendary. Wherever he went, no matter how much he had to drink the night before, his suitcase was immaculately packed with his clothes all neatly folded. He even used those things that keep your shoes in shape when you're not wearing them. I used to stuff all my gear in the case and sit on it to close it.

It was a shame that Ron Greenwood, the West Ham manager, didn't always see eye-to-eye with Bobby. Ron was a fantastic manager and a great coach and his training was miles ahead of everyone else's at that time, but Bobby always used to say one thing about him. 'Do you know, Harry, that in all my time with West Ham Ron never ever said "well done" or "well

31

played" to me. Not once.' That was Bobby's big regret. Ron didn't show his feelings. Bobby told me while we were in America together that even though he had captained England to a World Cup triumph the one thing he needed most from Greenwood was an occasional pat on the back. 'We all need that, no matter who we are', Bobby told me. And that's one thing I've carried into management. Players need to be congratulated by their manager if they've performed well. By the same token if they've played crap I'll tell them that as well.

Ron was the same with me, with all the players, as he was with Bobby. But he couldn't have had an easy time with us. We were a right bunch of lads, not easy to control. I look back now and wonder how we got away with half the things we did. One night we were confined to our rooms after a shambolic display at Stoke. Ron was livid with our performances and wouldn't let us out. But some of us sneaked out of the window and made our way to a nightclub, not getting back until about four in the morning. As we climbed over a fence to get back into the hotel, Bobby slipped and landed on a spike, and it took us ages to free him. The next morning we had to keep a limping Bobby out of Ron's sight on the train home, and when we reported back to the ground later that afternoon Bobby said he'd tripped in his garden and landed on a fence. He was out for the next two weeks.

Fans who remember Bobby's style of play will recall him getting the ball from his keeper, or the full back, and chipping it forward for Geoff Hurst. He initiated attacks, both for West Ham and England. But the man most responsible for Bobby's style was none other than Malcolm Allison. Malcolm was The Guv'nor at West Ham when Bobby arrived. He was one of the players but used to help out coaching the kids twice a week. Malcolm was a very strong character and very flamboyant. I remember him coming into the dressing room one day and cutting the sleeves off the team shirts and the legs from the shorts. He'd been over to Holland to check out coaching methods and saw how modern the strips were over there. He was always ahead of his time.

When Bobby first went to West Ham he was almost the last choice to get taken on. He wasn't a superstar schoolboy. But Malcolm really believed in Bobby and Bobby in him, although sometimes Malcolm had a strange way of showing it. One day Bobby was marking a kid from Chelsea called Barry Bridges, probably the best youth player in the country. Bobby followed Bridges all over the field, hardly getting a kick of the ball, but because his opponent hadn't done much either, Bobby felt he was due a pat on the back from Malcolm. But he had a shock in store.

'If I ever see you play like that again, I'll never speak to you again,' Malcolm told Bobby. 'You were never available for a pass from your keeper, never dropped square for your full back. I never saw you kick the ball. You'll never be a player if you don't take responsibility and want the ball.' Malcolm absolutely slaughtered him, but from then on his whole game changed, and he went on to become one of the greatest players in the history of the game.

Bobby died from bowel cancer on 23 February 1993 after a long illness, but for so long no one apart from his family knew he was ailing. He never told a soul. Even when his illness was getting too much for him he never felt sorry for himself. I know there was plenty written in the newspapers about Bobby's first wife, Tina, putting his World Cup winner's medal and other trophies up for sale, but I'm sure Bobby would have wanted that. He wasn't the kind of feller to show off with his medals – he'd much rather Tina and his kids Dean and Roberta see something out of them.

He spent a few days in Bournemouth with me towards the end of his life and we went to watch the horses working at racehorse trainer David Elsworth's yard. Not once did Bobby complain that things were getting too much to him. He'd go for his treatment to a clinic in Scotland and not say a word to anyone. I remember when I went to see him after he'd had his operation. I could have cried. Bobby was always a big lad, big legs, a powerful build, but suddenly his trousers were hanging off him at the back because he'd lost so much weight. It slaughtered me to see him like that. He'd say to me he was doing okay but he knew all along he wasn't. He knew what was coming but faced it with incredible bravery. That was how he was – unflappable. You couldn't help but love him.

In my eyes he was every kid's hero. I have a picture of him on my office wall. In it he's only 10, playing for Barking schoolboys. There he is, the team captain, those blond locks flowing, collecting the trophy. Looking at it you can almost imagine that even at that tender age he knew his destiny was to go on and captain his country to win the greatest trophy in the world. He lived the dream of every kid. And he was lovely with it. It was impossible not to want to be in his company. All the famous stars such as Jimmy Tarbuck and Sean Connery loved to be with Mooro, too. In fact, Tarbuck spoke at his memorial service at Westminster Abbey in July 1993 and really moved everyone there. He spoke from the heart and you knew how much he loved Bobby. 'Win or lose, on the booze,' was Mooro's motto, Tarbuck told everyone, and it was true. Bobby knew his responsibilities on the football field, but he had such a marvellous zest for life off it.

While Bobby Moore was the big star at West Ham, Geoff Hurst and Martin Peters also had their share of the limelight because of their England accomplishments. They were both lovely fellers but they kept themselves to themselves a lot more than Bobby. They mixed in different circles. Martin had a fantastic talent for scoring goals. He was an 18-goal-a-year man, which was terrific from midfield. He could play anywhere, in goal, defence, midfield, up front. In many ways he was similar to Bryan Robson. Not as aggressive as Robbo of course, but like Robbo he had the knack of getting into the box and scoring important goals from midfield.

Geoff was a terrific player also, a striker respected the world over after his famous World Cup Final hat-trick – everywhere, that is, apart from America. When Geoff and I played together late in our careers for Seattle Sounders, Geoff was given something of a hard time. The fans there had loved the striker who preceded him, a feller called John Rowlands, who spent most of his career in the lower divisions in England, and they didn't take too well to Geoff. One day after a game a Seattle supporter approached Geoff and said: 'Hey, Hurst, you're no good. Rowlands was twice the player.' It was a serious comment but I didn't know whether to laugh or cry. After all, this was the only guy to score a hat-trick in the World Cup Final they were talking to. But Geoff took it in his stride, as he always did, and just smiled. I was delighted to hear of Geoff's knighthood – it's thoroughly deserved but it won't change him one little bit. He will still be the bubbly, down-to-earth character he's always been.

Martin was almost an established star at West Ham when I arrived in 1963, and I never really got to know him as well as Geoff. He was a few years older than me, but he was on the same youth trip as me to Holland to play in the Blau Wit tournament, a prestigious competition for under-19s that always attracted the youth sides from the top clubs in Holland and around Europe. I'd only left school a week and, at 15, I was there only for the ride. There was no question of me playing. We were all due to be farmed out to local Dutch families who would look after us for the duration of the tournament. I'd never been away from home in my life, never out of the country, so this was a big trip for me. It had been arranged that I would stay with a Dutch couple called Eddie and Ikje Oostergaard, and when my name was read out on arrival in Amsterdam, Eddie was there to meet me. All the rest of the lads had been driven away in big cars but Eddie had come to pick me up on his moped. It must have looked a comical sight. Eddie, wearing spectacles that looked like the bottom of beer bottles, beetling his moped through Amsterdam, with me holding on to him for dear life with one hand and trying desperately to manage my suitcase and bag with the other. 'What am I doing here?' I thought. 'This can't be happening.'

Before we'd left the airport it had been arranged that we should all meet at 8pm that night in the main square. But by the time I'd wobbled through Amsterdam at 12 miles per hour on the back of Eddie's moped and settled in to my temporary home, I was running late. I got to the meeting point at 8.15pm, by which time all the lads had disappeared. To be honest that was no surprise. I was a fresh-faced kid straight out of school while most of the other lads had been on the staff at West Ham for a few years. Few of them probably even knew I was on the trip. So I started walking around Amsterdam, a 15-year-old who'd hardly set foot outside East London, hunting for the rest of the West Ham contingent. There was no sign of them. I even began to look in nightclubs and got chased down a street by a bouncer, great big geezer, who must have thought I was trying to bunk into his club. Well I hope that was the reason. My spirits were beginning to flag when I realized with absolute horror that I did not know the address of Eddie's home. I did not know where I was and I did not know where I was staying. Not a clue. Bloody hell. By this time it was almost midnight and I was close to tears. Suddenly I spotted a boy called Roger Hugo, one of the older players in the squad. I told him my dilemma and he took me back to his digs for the night. Needless to say, Eddie and Ikje had sent out a search party for me. They were scouring Amsterdam searching for this young Londoner. But it all got sorted out the next day.

Eddie and Ikje had told all their friends and neighbours that they had this West Ham footballer staying with them, and every day Eddie would say to me: 'You play today, Harry?'

'No,' I'd say, 'I'm not playing.'

'So you are the substitute then?'

'No. I'm not substitute,' and Eddie would walk away

shaking his head, bewildered that he was putting up the only budding footballer who never played any football. But West Ham wanted to win the tournament so they would always play their best team and consequently I never got a look-in. The following year I went to Amsterdam again to represent the England youth team. I'd kept in touch with Eddie and his wife to let them know how I was getting on, but hadn't been in contact for a few months. So while we were in the city I took Howard Kendall, one of my England team-mates, to call on Eddie. He was shocked to see me, but even more shocked when I told him that I was with England, and that I WAS PLAYING!

'You play!' he said, wide-eyed with amazement.

I got Eddie and his family and friends tickets for the final in which we beat Spain 4–0, and he was thrilled.

At the risk of sounding big-headed, I was a top-notch player at youth level. I played for East London Schoolboys and as a young teenager I had the pick of all the London clubs. It's perhaps fair to say I was one of the most sought-after teenagers in the country. In those days the scouts would be around your house every other night, sitting there for a few hours talking to you and your parents about football. One night Chelsea, the next night Spurs, and so on. One night I was playing football around the blocks of flats that backed onto the council estate where I lived. I looked around and walking towards me was Wilf Chitty, the chief scout for Chelsea, and Tommy Docherty, the Chelsea manager. This was raising the stakes a bit, having the manager coming round. The Doc told me that if I signed for Chelsea I'd be pushing for a first-team place at 18 because he liked to bring in the younger players. I'd watched the Doc play for Arsenal and to me he was someone a bit special, a real character.

At the same time, Bill Nicholson wanted me to join Tottenham, but Ron Greenwood at West Ham had an edge. He started inviting my mum and dad and me to Hammers youth matches. My mum had never been to a football match and she liked the feeling at West Ham, she felt at home there. We all recognized the club as a place where youth got its chance. It was a family club, not like Arsenal which was a team of big-spenders. Spurs was a bit of a cheque-book team too, and Chelsea was a bit out of the way, despite the lure of the Doc. But West Ham always produced its own players, it had a great youth policy. So I joined Hammers as an apprentice, in 1963, and sure enough we won the FA Youth Cup the first year I was there. We played Liverpool in the final and lost the first leg 3–1. At half-time, in the return leg at Upton Park, we were 2–1 down, making it 5–2 on aggregate. But we ended up winning 6–5 on a never-to-be-forgotten night. We had a centre forward called Martin Britt who gave Tommy Smith, the Anfield Iron, a real battering. And believe me that took some doing. Martin was fantastic in the air. He was like a man playing against kids, and with me supplying crosses from the right wing and John Sissons from the left, Martin scored four goals. There were 25,000 at Upton Park that night and they all went mad. Ron Greenwood said it was the best night of his life. Martin Britt was in the first team at West Ham by the time he was 18 but was soon afterwards sold to Blackburn and a bad knee injury wrecked his career.

The following season we had 10 of that same Cup-winning side in the youth team and we were odds-on certainties to retain the trophy. In fact we were so good that nine of the team made it to the final Probables v Possibles trial for England Youth. I don't know whether we were complacent but we were beaten by Arsenal, who had the likes of John Radford and Peter Storey playing.

I made my first-team debut for Hammers, aged 19, in the 1965–66 season, the season that was to finish so memorably for Moore, Hurst and Peters. It was against Sunderland, who had just signed the great Jim Baxter from Rangers, at Upton Park on a Monday night. We'd lost 3–0 at West Brom two days earlier in the first match of the season. We drew 1–1 against the

Rokermen, with Martin Peters heading home my corner in the fourth minute to put us ahead. A few days later, on the Saturday, we beat Leeds, the start of the great Leeds team, 2–0.

I didn't find the step-up to the first team any problem. I always believed I had the ability as a winger to beat any full-back and the punters loved me. Things went great for me early on and the Hammers were doing okay. But somehow I never fulfilled at the highest level the potential I had shown so often on the youth stage. Looking back I know I should have done better, but the game was changing a lot then. Full backs suddenly weren't slow any more. Now they were as quick as the wingers. In the old days if you were slow you played full back. Now it was a new era of thinking. The full backs were getting tight to wingers, not giving you a yard to control the ball. Suddenly whenever you got the ball you were clattered within a split second. It was getting harder and harder to play in that position, unless you played in a dominant team which enjoyed a lot of possession and could feed the winger regularly. We were wingers pure and simple. We stayed out wide, never came in, and were expected to do something with the ball on the few occasions we got it. Suddenly wingers died out, as Sir Alf Ramsey underlined with his England World Cup side. As my form dipped so did my popularity at Upton Park. My confidence was draining and for a long spell the punters hated me. And Upton Park was a difficult place to play if you were a winger. A section of the ground called the Chicken Run was right on top of you, the crowd could almost touch you, and every time you got the ball they expected you to turn the full back inside out and get a cross in.

In those days Leeds were the team to beat. They were a fantastic side and very difficult to play against. But in a funny way I enjoyed our meetings because I always seemed to get the better of Leeds left-back Terry Cooper. Terry was a great player, but because he had such attacking instincts he'd often forget about defending and leave me plenty of room to do some damage. I always fancied my chances against Terry, always gave him a hard time. I remember getting sent off at Leeds one time and the more I think of it the more I realize it was a set-up. Leeds were a great side but they were also very cynical and if a player was causing them damage, they'd find ways to deal with him. Leeds had the likes of Billy Bremner, Johnny Giles, Norman Hunter, Jack Charlton, Eddie Gray, Paul Reaney, and up front Allan Clarke and Mick Jones. They could stand shoulder to shoulder with the best British teams of any generation. This one Saturday, in October 1968, I started superbly. I went past Cooper time after time inside the first 15 minutes and God knows how the scoreline was still 0–0. I won a corner after one jinking run and Bremner complained loudly to the referee that it was a goal-kick. 'Stop moaning. You're always f****** moaning', I said to him. As we lined up for the corner Bremner stamped on my foot and I pushed him away. Next second he raked his studs down my shin. I reacted by kicking him and he went down like he was dead. Suddenly I had nine Leeds players surrounding me, jostling me, looking to strangle me.

The only West Ham player amid the melee, apart from me, was Billy Bonds, trying to come to my rescue. I got my marching orders and as I trooped towards the Elland Road tunnel, I passed close to Mooro, who had stayed in the other half of the pitch. I'll never forget that look on his face. He had his arms folded and made a gesture with his hands as if to say 'Oh Harry boy, what have you gone and done now?' But that was a shrewd Leeds tactic. I'd been playing well and they suckered me into retaliation. I was suspended as a result of the Leeds sending-off and in those days you didn't get paid if you were under suspension. Bill organized a whip-round for me and even asked Ron Greenwood to contribute. Ron was so embarrassed about being asked that he coughed up. I'd acted stupidly, cost West Ham the game, and there was Ron putting into the whip for me. The following week we beat Sunderland 8–0 at Upton Park. Geoff Hurst scored a hat-trick in each half and I think I made about five of them. Mooro and Trevor Brooking netted the other two.

I think the beginning of the end for me at West Ham came a month into the start of the 1970–71 season, a season which saw us fail to win a match until 3 October and ultimately finish third from bottom, just above the relegated Burnley and Blackpool. We were at home to Newcastle and playing absolutely terribly. Trevor Brooking was sub, and after we went 1–0 down Ron Greenwood wanted to bring him on. I was about the only Hammers player doing anything and I couldn't believe it when I realized it was me Ron wanted to bring off. To show my disgust I walked as slowly as I could across the pitch towards the tunnel – I must have taken about two minutes – and the crowd were booing the decision to replace me. After the game, which we lost 2–0, I was sitting in the medical room when Ron walked up to me and said angrily: 'Don't you ever do that to me again. When I pull you off you run off, you don't walk.' But I wasn't standing for it. 'And don't you f***** do that to me again either. It's always me isn't it? It could have been any of the 11 of us but you had to pick me.' Ron stormed out of the room. As he did I picked up a bottle of lager – Jimmy Greaves and Mooro were having a drink – and smashed it against the door he'd just walked through.

'You're a nice one, Harry,' Greavesie shouted.

'Oh don't you start,' I said.

'Well,' he said, 'you could have picked up an empty one. That was our last lager, wasn't it Mooro?'

After that incident, I guess not surprisingly, I rarely got a look-in again with Ron.

I was a professional footballer with a London club in the swinging Sixties but to be honest I never got trapped in the web of glamour. That was for the likes of George Best. We'd get invitations to all sorts of places because of Mooro's image, and he always liked to take me and Frank Lampard along because he liked our company, but I preferred being in the East End. We'd go to TV shows like *Top Of The Pops* and mix with the girls from Pan's People, but it was never really my scene. I was more at home at my local pub the Blind Beggar, in Whitechapel, where Ronnie Kray shot George Cornell. They were great days at West Ham, but injuries and loss of form were to cut short my playing career there, and it was my old mate John Bond, a former favourite at West Ham, who was to take me to Bournemouth for £31,000 in the summer of 1972.

Bournemouth were going places at the time. The chairman was a man called Harold Walker, who was pumping a fortune into the club and Bondy was spending it. He had top players like Ted MacDougall and Phil Boyer at the club, and signed me and ex-Everton star Jimmy Gabriel on the same day.

Bondy had gone to Bournemouth as manager by a complete fluke. He was at a loose end when his playing career finished, at West Ham, and Frank Lampard and I, to help out an old mate, threw a bit of work his way. Four afternoons a week we'd coach the kids at a local school in Canning Town, and cut Bondy into the nice little sideline, splitting our shifts three ways. He was a bit older than us, was Bondy, but we'd always counted him as a mate. One afternoon he told us he'd applied for the assistant manager's job at Bournemouth. In those days they appointed assistants separately from managers, not like today when a new manager would take with him all his backroom staff. Cyril Lee, who was Bobby Robson's right-hand man at Ipswich, was expected to fill the post, but for some reason he never made it to the interview with Walker, the multi-millionaire. Walker was impressed from the word go with Bondy, and when Lee failed to show up he made Bond the manager. So from one minute being unemployed Bondy found himself manager of one of the most up-and-coming clubs in the country.

Bondy had made an early attempt to lure me from West Ham but at that stage I didn't fancy going from the top flight down into the lower divisions. I'd made 149 League appearances for Hammers, scoring seven goals, plus one goal from 26 cup appearances. But as it became clearer I was out of the picture at West Ham, I decided a move would be in my best interests and I signed for Bournemouth in the summer of 1972. Within 18 months of me joining the Cherries, Bondy had moved to take over as manager of Norwich, who were in the First Division, and he wanted to take me to Carrow Road with him too. But a niggling knee injury had steadily got worse and by the time Bondy tried to sign me, I could hardly run. He was upset with his replacement at Bournemouth, Trevor Hartley, for trying to flog him an injured player, and suggested I joined Norwich on loan. But the loan period didn't work out. My knee got worse and I was in plaster for three months hoping torn tendons would knit together.

I officially retired in 1976, aged 29, my knee no longer able to withstand the rigours of professional football in England. But I was able to play at a lower level, specifically in America, and it was there that I was lured by my ex-Bournmouth team-mate Jimmy Gabriel later that year, first as player and then as coach. It should have been the American Dream but it turned into a Yankee Nightmare.

CHAPTER 3

The American Nightmare

Being from the East End of London, I like to think that I'm as street-wise as they come, but that didn't stop me falling victim to the most outrageous con-man I've ever come across during my time in the United States in the late 1970s. Looking back now I console myself with the fact that I recognized the early signs of a con, that the Redknapp alarm bells had sounded, but somehow I allowed myself to be smooth-talked by the fastest tongue in the West.

Jimmy Gabriel and I had hit it off while playing together at Bournemouth. We lived close to one another and would drive to training every day together. When Jimmy left Bournemouth he went out to America to join Seattle Sounders in what at that time was a thriving football environment. Jimmy must have respected my coaching technique because before he left for the States he told me he'd love to have me over there as coach. In March 1976, Seattle appointed Jimmy as coach and the first thing he did was get me over, first as a player but ultimately to assist him on the coaching staff. So later that month I gave up life in England and took my wife Sandra and my two young boys Mark and Jamie to begin a new life in America. I loved it out there. Football, or soccer as they called it, was flying. Bobby Moore came out to join Jimmy and I. So too Geoff Hurst, Mike England, Alan Hudson, and Jimmy Robertson, the old Tottenham player. So we had a really good side. We averaged 28,000 for our home games, which gives you some idea how popular the game was in the States then. My first game for Seattle was against the New York Cosmos in a new stadium called the Kingdome and the gate was an incredible 66,000. I'd like to think I had something to do with such a large crowd but I reckon a guy by the name of Pele, who was playing for Cosmos along with Franz Beckenbauer, may be due a certain amount of credit. He was different class, even though his best years had long gone. They beat us 3–1, but the game really gave me an appetite for the months ahead.

Me, Bobby Moore and Geoff Hurst and our families all had apartments in the same complex and the lifestyle was fantastic. We would go training in the mornings and our wives would go to the nearby lake to get a barbecue ready. We'd finish training at 1pm, go to the lake, have a swim, and play with the kids until about 8pm. It was one long holiday really, for six months of the year. The fans treated us like superstars. And there was never any hint of violence. In England football at the time was still scarred by hooliganism, but in America going to soccer was all about having a good time. Fans would open up the back of their cars or vans and they'd stand there outside the stadium before a game cooking hamburgers and having a drink. It was great. And the money was decent too. This was still paradise time. The nightmare was still to come.

Things had gone really well for Seattle. We got to the North American Soccer League play-off final against the Cosmos in 1977, but they beat us 2–1. I think we could almost have won but unfortunately we had a deaf goalkeeper called Tony

Chursky, whose disability cost us victory in the most comic of circumstances. Cosmos striker Steve Hunt chased our keeper to a loose ball near the by-line. The keeper won the challenge and, thinking Hunt was still yards behind him on the ground, began to dribble it out of his area. Then the pantomime began. Hunt had crept back onto the pitch and was stealthily making ground on Tony. We're all shouting: 'Tony, he's behind you', but he couldn't hear a bleeding word. Hunt then nicked the ball off him and put it in the net.

During this time in the late Seventies, I was spending six months of the year back in England. I'd keep myself fit playing for non-League sides like AP Leamington, but I'd also keep an eye out for players to take back to the States. One of the players I lured back during this time was Alan Hudson, something of a coup considering he was still only about 28 at the time. Alan was out of favour at Arsenal and I was due to meet him at Heathrow Airport to sign forms and stuff like that. Arsenal manager Terry Neill was there and after the deal was completed Terry went to shake hands with Alan.

'F*** off,' Huddy said to him, and started to give him the most fearful abuse you've ever heard in your life.

'Oh no,' I thought. 'What have I done signing this geezer?' To be honest it was very embarrassing. I didn't know where to put myself, but all credit to Terry Neill, he just stood there and took it before walking off. So I feared the worst when I took Huddy back to the States but he was as good as gold. He was such a talented footballer it was unbelievable but, boy, could he drink. He could go out after a game and drink all night, all the next day, then come in for training the next morning and leave everyone for dead. Whatever work he did it wasn't enough. I've never ever seen anyone train like Huddy. All that booze he drank and he never ever put any weight on because he never ate. He would train, play and booze. Alan had a very serious accident in 1997 and I think it was only his levels of fitness, even now after years out of the game, that kept him alive. He was knocked down by a car and his injuries were horrific, a near miracle that he survived. His road to recovery has been slow and painful, but it will be lovely to see Alan up and about again because he's a real character.

That last year at Seattle, in 1979, didn't go so well for us and when Jimmy got an offer to go to Phoenix in Arizona, he was keen to move. It was a five-year contract on fantastic money. The only trouble was that Phoenix were not in the North American Soccer League, which by now had players of the calibre of Cruyff, Best and Gerd Muller, but a new league called the American Soccer League, strictly second division stuff. Jimmy had been told that Phoenix would be in the Mickey Mouse League for only one year while they got over teething problems and from then would be guaranteed a place in the NASL.

'It's all sorted,' Jimmy told me. 'But they want you to join me; it'll be me and you as a team again. The main man's going to ring you tonight to sort out a deal.'

That night the phone rang.

'Harry,' an American accent drawled, 'Len Lesser here. I'm the president of the Phoenix Fire. We're starting a new soccer team here in Phoenix and we want you and Jimmy Gabriel to be our Dream Team. You've proved you can do it at Seattle; now we want you to do the same here in Phoenix.'

I asked him about terms and he offered me the silliest money I've ever heard in my life. Five-year contract. Mega-money. 'And what about the good wife?' he went on. 'What car would she like? No doubt a convertible?' Of course, I said, even though Sandra's never passed her driving test. We'll give you a housing allowance, he went on, so many thousand dollars a month. You can buy a beautiful home for your family in Phoenix.

Now, I'd never made any dough out of football, so this offer from the Phoenix Fire really made the mouth water even though looking back the ridiculously generous terms should have made me suspicious. So we left Seattle to head back to England for a few months before returning to our new challenge in Phoenix.

'We'll start paying you right away,' Lesser had told me, 'but instead of sending the money over to England, we'll keep it here for you for when you return.'

Jimmy told me the first thing we had to do was get some players so while I was back in England I signed three players. I'd thought to myself if I'm going to spend another five years away from home, I'll surround myself with mates. Good players, but lads I could have a good laugh with. I knew the league was hardly going to be top-level stuff. First up was a lad called Neil Hague who was a mate of mine at Bournemouth but who by this time was playing for Darlington. He lived life to the full did Haguey, a real lad.

'Haguey,' I said down the phone. 'Fancy coming to America?'

He was a real poseur. Put him anywhere in the sun and the shades were out, he was that kind of feller. 'You're winding me up', he said. I convinced him I wasn't and that there was a three-year contract on the table, but I was concerned that Darlington wouldn't release him.

'They'll release me,' he said. 'I'll strangle the manager if they don't.'

I was beginning to feel like Yul Brynner in *The Magnificent Seven*, rounding up a band of gringos to fight beside me. Next was a boy called Keiron Baker, who at the time was a goalkeeper on Ipswich's books. And I also called on Terry Shanahan, later to join me as assistant at Bournemouth.

So we were all together on the plane to Phoenix, all our families in tow. The lads couldn't believe their luck. They'd all come from God knows where and now they were off to play in America for three years on great money. However, on the first day there I had a meeting with Len Lesser, during which I began to harbour suspicions. He had taken me and Jimmy out for a meal, but when the bill came I saw him messing about with it. I tried to see what he was doing and spotted him altering the bill from $40 to $240 after he'd settled it. I thought to myself 'what's this geezer up to – he's supposed to own the bleedin' club?' What I didn't know at the time was that he'd persuaded five investors to stump up $500,000 each to finance this great new Phoenix adventure. I whispered to Jimmy: 'Jimmy, there's something about this geezer. I don't like him.' But Jimmy would have none of it. He was always a bit naive, was Jimmy. Hard to believe about a tough Scot who'd spent so much time on Merseyside playing for Everton, but he gave everyone the benefit of the doubt. He would never see any harm in anyone. 'No, Harry,' he said. 'This guy's brilliant. Just give him a chance.'

The following night we were preparing for our first game against Chicago Sting, which drew a crowd of 10,000. A sell-out. Everything was ready, all the players were fit and raring to go, but the kit hadn't turned up. Half an hour to kick-off and still no sign of the kit. With 10 minutes left it finally materialized. I was like a madman throwing shirts and shorts out to all the players when it suddenly dawned on me that there was no goalkeeper's jersey.

'Len,' I said. 'There's no keeper's jersey for Keiron. He's got the same shirt as the rest of the team.'

'That's right, Harry,' he said. 'We're going to be the smartest team in the League. None of this bullshit with players wearing different uniforms. I want us all to have the same uniform.'

It took me 10 minutes to explain to this idiot that the keeper had to wear a different shirt. He'd obviously never watched a football match before in his life.

'No Harry, I hear what you say, but we're all going to wear the same uniform.'

By now I was at my wit's end. 'He bleedin' can't wear the same shirt. He picks the ball up, the others kick it, he has to wear a different shirt.'

Anyway Keiron wore somebody's jumper and played his part in our win, but broke his arm while making a save. It wasn't a great start for him, but he spotted what I'm sure he thought would be a silver lining. There wasn't a decent sports shop in Phoenix, at least one where we could get proper football boots, shin pads and the like. So, as Keiron was due to fly home to pick up his wife Tricia, who was pregnant back in Bournemouth and hadn't flown out with us initially, we put our orders in with him to bring gear back from England. Forty pairs of boots, plus a load of other gear on top. He must have thought he'd had it off. He knew Ted MacDougall had a sports shop in Bournemouth and that he'd get a massive discount. He must have counted on earning himself about $600, after he'd claimed back the expenses from Lesser.

Before he returned I went to the bank in Phoenix to withdraw some money. It was my birthday, 2 March, and I wanted to take Sandra and the kids out for a good night. I'd put £5,000 of my own money in the bank, and I had the back-pay Phoenix Fire owed me. That's what I thought, anyway, as I approached the counter.

'I'm sorry Sir, there's no money in this account.'

A hollow feeling began to hit me in the pit of my stomach. I asked the cashier to check again and she gave me the same response. 'Shall I call the manager, Sir?'

The manager came out and explained to me that earlier that morning he'd closed the Phoenix Fire account because it was $750,000 overdrawn. As I was being paid by the club, my money had been reclaimed. I think I realized at that very moment what Lesser had been up to. After a bit of arguing the manager admitted he'd made a mistake and that the £5,000 I'd deposited of my own money should be paid to me. But that was small comfort. Everything had gone belly-up.

I walked out of the bank to the car where Sandra and the boys were waiting and she could tell by the look on my face that something was horribly wrong. I told her what had happened as I gunned the car towards the Phoenix Fire stadium for a confrontation with Lesser. I rang Jimmy to let him know, only to find out from his wife that all their cheques had bounced at the supermarket. Jimmy and I met at the ground and stormed in to Lesser's office. We found him sitting there beneath a giant photo of himself and American President Jimmy Carter playing golf together.

'What's going on?' I demanded.

'Gee, Harry, it's great to see you and Jimmy, our very own super-coaches.'

'Never mind all that. What's happened to our money? The bank says all the cheques have bounced.'

'Oh gee,' he said. 'I know what's happened there. I've just transferred one and a half million dollars from one account to another. Yeah, I can see what the problem is. Don't worry about it, I'll sort it all out on Monday.'

'But I was going to take Sandra and the children out tonight for my birthday,' I said. 'I've got no money.'

'Don't worry, Harry, don't worry,' he said, reaching into his wallet. 'Here's 20 bucks.'

'20 bucks!' I said, disgusted. 'I'm going out for dinner, not a f****** McDonald's.'

Sure enough by Monday the whole thing had gone up the wall. Lesser had spirited away all the money put up by the five investors, a cool $2,500,000, in a classic con, but he never did a runner, he just stood there and faced us all. He was going to get nicked and he knew it, but he'd hidden all the money away. He was sitting there in front of us all taking everything we threw at him. He was incredible. It turned out he'd been done for something similar before. But he turned up in Phoenix, managed to persuade these five investors to hand over their cash by boasting he'd signed up Jimmy Gabriel and Harry Redknapp, who guided the Sounders to the Championship final with the Cosmos, and took all their money. And we were part of the con. Lesser was unreal. How he had the nerve to sit there and face us all I'll never know. The picture of him with Jimmy Carter was a con too – it was Jimmy Carter's head on the body of Lesser's mate!

'Guys, he said, 'I can't believe this has happened. I've got these super-coaches Jimmy and Harry…'

But he got no further. I called him all sorts. 'We don't want to hear all this crap. Where's our dough? We want our dough.' But there was no dough. He'd pocketed it all and had no intention of giving any of it back.

Meantime Keiron was on his way back from England, with 40 pairs of boots in tow. We met him at the airport. 'Harry, I've got the boots,' he said with a big beaming smile. 'Keiron,' I said. 'We've got the boots, but we haven't got a team.' Poor guy. He had his wife with him who was nine months' pregnant and 40 pairs of football boots which he'd paid for and suddenly it had all fallen around his ears. It looked as if he wasn't even going to get paid for the boots.

By this time the club had claimed the cars back from all the players. The only one they hadn't got was mine, and I had no intention of handing it back. We needed the car to ferry all the boys and their wives to the airport. So the car-hire people were trying to trace me, and I was moving from hotel to hotel to evade them. The lads I took over to the States were gutted but they knew I wasn't to blame. I'd been just as badly hit as them.

Lesser eventually got done for the con. Jimmy had to testify in court against him but in the days leading up to his court appearance he got cold feet.

'Harry, I feel bad about this,' he said.

'Feel bad?' I said, astonished. 'You get along to that court and get him banged up for life.' In the end Lesser got put away for two years.

By this time, going back to Seattle was no longer an option because they'd changed all their staff. Mark and Jamie were playing football for a kids team called the Phoenix Firebirds, run by one of the investors who'd done his money to Lesser. He was a guy called Tom Sidero, a builder who was striking it rich because building was taking off like mad in Phoenix. Tom gave us a house to live in which we shared with Terry Shanahan, later to join me at Bournemouth, and his wife Jackie.

We stayed while Tom tried to get the team reformed but it was always going to be difficult. Our future was very much up in the air at the time until a phone call from my old mate Bobby Moore took me back to England and another year of hell.

CHAPTER 4

Life's a Bowl of Cherries

It's hard to imagine Bobby Moore, captain of England's World Cup winning team in 1966 and one of the most respected men in soccer, struggling to eke out a living in the twilight world of non-League football.

But it was a message from Bobby, in the summer of 1980, then managing a little-known team called Oxford City, that brought me and my family back to England from the United States. Bobby and I had been big mates since our playing days together at West Ham and he'd always promised me that if ever he got a job in management, he'd want me beside him. He'd seen me in action as a coach at Seattle and I think he rated me highly. This was Bobby Moore, surely the kind of big name all the top clubs would be after. He was a banker to manage a First Division side. But, no, Bobby found himself at Oxford City, with me beside him. 'Let's give it a year, Harry,' he promised me. 'If we do all right we'll get fixed up okay.'

Oxford wanted me to work full-time and gave me my own company car. Sounds great, doesn't it, until you learn that the wages were £120 a week, my car was a little green Fiesta, and I was travelling up every day from Bournemouth, a journey of 120 miles. Bobby was on about £500 a week, but I didn't begrudge him that. He was Bobby Moore, for Christ's sake. The chairman was a guy called Tony Rosser, who had formerly been chairman at Oxford United. He'd had a big falling-out at United and decided to buy Oxford City. Rosser had big ambitions. He wanted to get Oxford City in the Football League and Oxford United out. That's why he signed up Bobby, it was all part of his master-plan. He spent an awful lot of money on the club and was bidding to buy a brand new training ground.

Bobby got a brand new Daimler from him, but my perks weren't quite so good. I was taken on full-time and given my office – a portakabin! I had to sit there all day, having driven up from Bournemouth, with nothing to do. There were no players – they were all at work of course. But Rosser insisted I was there because he had all these fancy plans. He wanted a professional outlook. Bobby would come for training two nights a week and of course for the games. But at least three times a week, twice for training and once or twice for a match, I'd be stuck in this portakabin all day, then I'd have to work with the players. By the time that was over it was about 9.30pm, followed by a bit of messing about, and then the drive all the way back to Bournemouth to get home for midnight. The next day I was up at the crack of dawn again driving up to Oxford. All for £120 a week.

To say we found it hard at Oxford is an understatement. I'd just come back from America and was totally out of touch with the game; Bobby didn't know a single player at that level either. I used to sit there thinking to myself 'What the hell am I doing here?' Then we would play somebody like Tilbury away in the pouring rain and I'd look to Bobby and think. 'What am *I* doing here? What is *he* doing here?'

Given Bobby's involvement, everybody wanted to beat us and it pains me to say we really saw the nasty side of some people's characters. Opposing teams would score a goal and make sure they ran from the other end of the pitch right to our dug-out to jump up and down in Bobby's face.

We were like fish out of water – neither of us could find the players. Bobby and I made the mistake of signing players from the Football League who'd reached the end of their careers and giving them too much dough. They couldn't handle that level, playing on crap pitches, in poor quality games, and the team suffered. We did manage to get to the Oxford Cup Final but got stuffed 5–0, and by then we'd both had enough.

It looked like I'd be out of work but for a real stroke of luck. Dave Webb, the former Chelsea player, was manager at my old club Bournemouth and he offered me a coaching job back at Dean Court. It was perfect for me. The money was still poor, but at least it was home. I didn't have to drive to Oxford every day and I was back in League football, albeit the Fourth Division. I got on great with Dave, who is a real larger-than-life character, and in my first year back we got promotion to Division Three. The only problem we had was that Webby has a self-destruct button somewhere in his head. Dave was into everything. He'd be buying cars, doing this and that, always chasing a pot of gold. He always thought he was too big for Bournemouth, that he should be manager of Chelsea. But could he pull some strokes!

I remember one night we were in a hotel before an away game. There was the chairman, vice-chairman, a couple of directors, Webby, me and a couple of others all round a table enjoying a meal. 'Watch this, Harry,' he whispered to me, before getting John Kirk, the Bournemouth physio, to persuade the girl on reception to announce on the pager: 'Telephone call for Mr Webb. Telephone call for Mr Webb. A Mr Bates on the line.' Webby took his time getting up from his chair, just long enough for Kirky to come rushing in. 'Dave,' he said. 'Ken Bates is on the phone for you.'

The chairman and directors looked at each other horrified. 'That's Ken Bates of Chelsea,' they gasped. I had to laugh. All Dave was doing was jacking up his wages another 15 grand a year and they couldn't see it. Dave had them all around his little finger. But he was never content with just managing a club. After six months he wanted to own it.

Comedian Jim Davidson joined the Bournemouth board in 1982 and we had the time of our lives. It was real laugh-a-minute stuff. I remember us winning at Stockport one day to go top of the league. On the way home our team coach and the Torquay United team coach were next to each other on the motorway. Torquay had the hump because we'd just gone above them, and as they passed, Jim Davidson stood up and did a moonie at them. This was a director of Bournemouth Football Club with his bare arse out of the window. It was fun and games all the way. During that time Jim put on shows in the supporters' club to raise funds. He had strippers in, the lot.

So things were going really well. That is until Webby pressed that button.

One night we were all having a night out at Lorenzo's, the restaurant in Bournemouth which I now own, and Webby was on the brandy. All of a sudden, without warning, he started giving it the large one. 'I'm too big for this club' he said.

'I shouldn't be at Bournemouth, I should be in control of Chelsea.'

'Oh do shut up, Webby,' I said. 'Do me a favour, just get on with the football. Why do you keep going on about owning a football club? You're doing well as manager, just stick to that.' Next day Webby was at the training ground wearing dark glasses, legless, still drinking brandy. 'I'm having a livener, Harry,' he said. 'A livener.' I just ignored him and took the players out training but quickly got a message from Kirky, the physio, that Webby wanted to see me. I said I'd be there after training but Kirky was insistent. 'You'd better come, Harry. Dave's in a mess.'

I went to see Dave, who by this time had many of the staff in his office with him – the groundsman, Kirky, almost everyone. 'Harry,' he began. 'I'm too big for this club. It's going nowhere. The chairman's got no ambition…' Just then the door opened and in walked the chairman. Webby's face was a picture. I've never seen anyone sober up so quickly. The chairman, Harold Walker, had heard everything. 'Oh, so you're too big for this club are you, Dave? You're going to resign are you? Okay, fine. We'll call it a day then.' And then he walked out of the room.

I was gutted. I thought if Dave was going, then I'd be on my bike too. I started to have a go at him, but he didn't seem in the least concerned. 'It'll be all right, H,' he said. That night Dave booked himself into a hotel in Bournemouth and invited me to join him. He had Jim Davidson arriving by helicopter and had hatched a plan to ring the chairman, with the support of me and Jim, to apologize. I was all for it because I couldn't afford to be out of work. The chairman was surprisingly okay about it. He was a nice man, Mr Walker, a solicitor and a multi-millionaire. He owned half of Bournemouth and you don't get that sort of dough for being a mug. But he swallowed what Dave had to say and everything was back to normal.

Things continued to go well. Webby had something about him. He wasn't great on the training ground but he could get players to play for him. He was a motivator, good in the dressing room, and fun to be around. I enjoyed his company very much, but before long his finger was hovering once more over that old self-destruct button. We were due to play Chesterfield and Dave had heard that our chairman was meeting two business acquaintances who were looking to put some money into the club. Dave by this stage was looking to take control of the club himself. He'd roped in Barry Briggs, a speedway rider, and a few other people who'd promised to invest money, and was a few quid short of 'having a coup,' as he liked to say. When the two potential directors pulled up in the car-park at noon on the Saturday, Dave was there in his own car waiting for them.

'Hello gentlemen,' he said. 'Dave Webb. I hear you're putting some money into the club.' They nodded, and Dave carried on. 'Well listen, don't put your dough in with Mr Walker. I'm having a coup, and Walker's going. Come in with me, I've got big plans.'

What Webby didn't know was that one of those two guys was Mr Walker's best friend from university days. The chairman got to know all about Webby's cloak-and-dagger conversation, and on the Monday told Dave he was finished. But for some reason I have never understood, he let Dave work until the Friday. Maybe Webby took this to mean that the chairman was just making an idle threat about sacking him because he didn't look too worried. We heard nothing more all week and on the Friday Webby rang the chairman. 'Hello Mr Walker. I've got a couple of terrific players I can get on free transfers. Could be worth a fortune in a couple of years. But it ain't worth me doing it if you meant what you said the other day.'

'Well you'd better not bother signing them,' said Walker, 'because I meant every word.' Dave looked like he had seen a ghost.

My fears that I'd be for the high jump if Dave left were unfounded. Bournemouth wanted me to take over as caretaker boss until they appointed a replacement. This was in December 1982 and my first game in charge was the following day.

We were away to Lincoln. And they were the League leaders.

Lincoln, managed by Colin Murphy, were flying at the time. They were the best footballing side in the division by a million miles. They had John Fashanu, Steve Thompson, who went on to manage Sheffield United, and really were different class. Now I'd love to say at this point that my first game as a fully-fledged manager (albeit a caretaker) was a roaring success, that we went to the League leaders, turned on a champagne performance, and stamped the name of H Redknapp in the minds of people. I'd love to say that. But if I did I'd be lying through my teeth.

Almost every game in the country was called off that day. A severe overnight frost made most grounds unplayable, and even as we travelled to Lincoln we knew the journey would be in vain because there was no way the match would go ahead. The Lincoln pitch was like concrete. No way could you play on it. But the ref somehow gave it the go-ahead. Kirky, the physio, got the boots out and I asked him where the ones with rubber studs were. 'We haven't got any,' he said. All we had were boots with long nylon studs, almost suicidal on a rock-hard-pitch. I couldn't believe it.

'Harry,' Kirky protested. 'I've been saying for weeks we needed new boots but no one would listen.' The Lincoln players came out with those boots with little pimples for studs, playing one-twos in the kick-about, pirouetting about like ballet dancers. We trundled out and right away three of our players went arse over tit. It was a joke. Looking back now you've got to laugh but I didn't see the funny side of it then. Crash, bang, wallop, we were 3–0 down at half-time. I said to Kirky: 'If we're not careful this could end up six or seven.' That was a bit optimistic as it turned out. The second half started and before I even reached the dug-out to sit down, Lincoln had scored a fourth. When the score got to seven we got a corner and Kirky shouted to our players to get forward. I roared louder at them to get back. 'What the hell are you playing at, Kirky?' I bellowed. 'Do you think we're going to win 8–7?' Lincoln scored their ninth with 18 minutes to go, so it could have easily reached 12 or 13. But luckily they eased off and it finished 9–0. We were lucky to get nil!

That's it, I thought, a short and not very sweet managerial career. I'll just wait for the new man to come in. But I was still in charge for our next match at Orient which we lost 5–0. What a start. Two games, 14 goals conceded, none scored. Look out Glenn Hoddle.

But once the shock of Webby's departure had subsided, results started to go our way. I remember we won at Reading and then went to Gillingham, who were second in the division, and won 5–1. On the coach on the way back Alec Stock, former Bournemouth manager and one of the directors, told me there was a board meeting the following Monday and that he would push for me to be given the manager's job. 'Write on a bit of paper what you need,' Alec told me. 'You know, car, petrol, telephone bill, bit more in your wages. And we'll see what we can do.'

But I was in for a bit of a shock. After the board meeting on the Monday the chairman, Mr Walker, popped his head round my door and told me he'd sold the club.

'I wasn't able to guarantee your position,' he said, 'but thanks for everything, and all the best for the future. Oh, by the way, the new people want to see you.' So that's what the board meeting was all about, I thought. Not to appoint me as new manager, just to hand over control of the club to a new group.

That was my first meeting with Brian Tiler, who was brought in as managing director by the new owner Anton Johnson. Anton was another larger-than-life character from the East End of London. He'd been a pop singer, had owned Rotherham Football Club, where he first met Brian, had owned night-clubs and was a real wheeler-dealer. The first time he turned up at the club he was wearing a full-length fur coat, and smoking a huge cigar. He drove a Rolls-Royce but it must have had about a million dents and was worth about tuppence. Yet that didn't stop him having his own chauffeur. Brian introduced himself to me, said that he'd heard great reports about me and that he wanted me to stay at the club, with Don Megson the new manager. In the meantime I'd been offered the assistant manager's job at Brighton by Jimmy Melia, and I'd heard one or two other clubs were considering approaching me, too. I told Brian I thought the time was right for me to leave Bournemouth but he was adamant that the new owners wanted me to stay on. 'See how it goes with Megson,' he said. 'I know he wants you to continue.' Meggie was a good bloke and I liked him. For a feller of more than 50 he was in great nick. He looked after himself, did Meggy.

A fortnight after the take-over Brian Tiler told me to get all the staff together for a night out, a getting-to-know-you session, all paid for by Anton. So I booked a restaurant at Bournemouth for about 20 of us.

'Have what you want lads,' Anton told us. 'Never mind the expense.'

The bill came at the end of the night and Anton said to his wife: 'Darling, hand me the cheque book.'

'I haven't got it,' she said. 'You had it last.'

'Oh blimey,' Anton said. 'I must have left it in Rotherham.'

So Brian and I had to foot the bill and I've never been paid back since. A couple of days later Anton asked me which members of staff had club cars. 'Tell them all to bring them to the ground tomorrow morning with the keys in,' he said. 'I want to buy them all new cars.' So the next day all the old cars were left in the car park only for Anton to flog them all, and before he had the chance to replace them he'd left the club. But you could not dislike the guy. At the end of the season he took us all to Portugal and we had a fantastic week. He was terrific company, Anton, a real character. He told me while we were in Portugal that he wanted to buy Southend United, but didn't know who to appoint manager. He asked me but I told him I didn't want to leave Bournemouth. 'Who can I get, then?' he asked. I said: 'Bobby's your man. Bobby Moore. Different class.' So Anton went ahead and bought Southend and gave Bobby the job. But Anton didn't stay long at Dean Court. He had interests everywhere and sold out to Rodney Barton and Peter McDonagh.

Things didn't go so well for Don Megson at Bournemouth. The team was struggling and he fell out in a big way with Brian and Anton. Brian used to give him some grief. I don't think he thought Meggy was up for the job. After about eight months Meggy got the bullet and in October 1984 I was back in charge, this time not as mere caretaker. 'We got it wrong when we first arrived,' Brian told me. 'We should have made you manager then.' We stayed up that season and then won the Associate Members Cup the following May. Unfortunately that was the only year the final wasn't played at Wembley. If I remember rightly the pitch had been cut up by the Horse Of The Year Show, so we ended up playing Hull in the final at their own ground.

My first signing at the start of my first full season was Colin Clarke. I went to see him play for Tranmere and I fancied him for my life. I told the chairman I wanted to buy him and the cost was £20,000 but the response was predictable. We didn't have that kind of money. But I knew Clarke could do a job for us so I got together a group of three mates – Tony Christofoli who owned a tiling company, Dave Smith who was a builder, and Norman Bishop who was a farmer – who were happy to back my judgement and we all agreed to chip in £5,000. I said to the chairman that my syndicate would buy Clarke for £20,000 for the club but that when we sold him we'd take any profit. That seemed to change his mind and all of a sudden the club found the funds to buy Clarke. Footballers nowadays get a bad name for lack of loyalty and what supporters see as mercenary attitudes but Clarke, an Irish lad and a big Chelsea fan, was terrific. The day I signed him we were sitting in my office waiting for forms to be completed when the phone rang. It was Colin's wife ringing from their hotel.

'Colin,' she said. 'Ian McNeill has been on the phone from Chelsea. They want you.' I couldn't believe it. We were 10 minutes away from completing the signing but Chelsea had been on and offered to triple whatever we had offered. 'Look

Dedicated follower of fashion. This is me in my typical football-watching gear, standing on the sidelines on a cold winter's day watching my dad play in the local Business Houses League.

Here's me (far left, front) with the East London Schoolboy's team. What a great side that was.

Hail the heroes... The West Ham youth team after beating Liverpool in the final of the FA Youth Cup in 1963. The handsome one, far left, is me. Then (from left), Colin Mackleworth, Dennis Burnett, John Charles, Bill Kitchener and Martin Britt.

Left: Another surging run from Redknapp. In action for the Hammers in February 1972.

Above: Here's me as a Bournemouth player – the glory days at Upton Park long gone.

'Say the Leeds and you're smiling.' I get my marching orders at Elland Road after a run-in with Billy Bremner in October 1968.

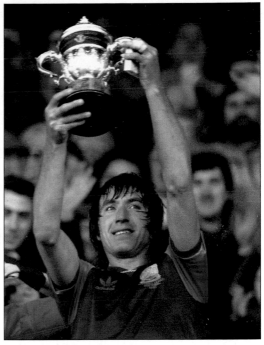

Above: Bobby Moore, in January 1964. He lived the dream of every schoolboy.

Above: Billy Bonds was a legend for West Ham during his playing days.

Below: Three of the all-time West Ham greats. Geoff Hurst, Bobby Moore and Martin Peters, pictured in 1966, contributed so much to England's World Cup triumph that year.

When Harry wed Sandra – and no that's not a betting slip the vicar's handing over.

Left: My nan, Maggie Brown, on my wedding day. It was from her that I inherited my gambling instincts.

Right: Sandra and I share a rare quiet moment at home in Bournemouth.

Happy families. In Bermuda with Sandra, Jamie and Mark, the night before Jamie's wedding.

*My mate Mooro, with his first wife Tina and daughter Roberta,
during our time in America. Mark is acting the goat alongside me.*

*Jamie – never without a ball – and Mark (far left) at a Seattle Sounders match in
August 1979.*

Left: Dad and lad.
I taught Jamie everything he knows.

Below: Piece of cake. Jamie and Louise after
an hour of wedded bliss in Bermuda.

Above: The daughter-in-law.
Also known as pop-star Louise and
the most down-to-earth girl you
could meet.

Above: Jamie in goalscoring form for
Liverpool. He's twice the player I ever was.

Memories of a lovely day. Frank and I in the winner's enclosure at Chepstow with my filly, Slick Cherry. We gave the bookies a good hiding that day!

Colin, I don't blame you,' I said. 'It's a good move for you. I'm just gutted that we were so close to getting you.' He looked at me for a minute and then said: 'Harry, I shook hands with you on the deal an hour ago and when I shake hands that's as good as my word. I'll still sign for you, but if in a year another club comes in for me with a good offer, you'll release me won't you?'

So Clarkie played for us for a season, got 36 goals, and then we sold him to Southampton for £500,000. My syndicate was gutted – that would have been a profit of almost half a million pounds – but at least it confirmed to me that I could spot a player and that I had a big future in this management game.

CHAPTER 5

Redknapp to the Rescue

I've a surprise for those Bournemouth fans who complained bitterly about the £100,000 pay-off I received from the club soon after my departure in the summer of 1992. When the Cherries looked like going out of business a few seasons ago, it was my money that saved the club.

It's something I've never spoken about before, but I just wanted to set the record straight and silence those critics who even now believe I in some way cheated the club. I must admit the reaction when news of my pay-out was broken hurt me. I'd put my life into Bournemouth and the money was no more than I deserved, yet Cherries fans couldn't disguise their anger. They argued that the money would have been better spent on reducing the club's mounting debt, which at that time was around £2.5 million.

But I was entitled to that £100,000 spread over four years. It was the remainder of my three-year contract. And I must have earned the club a fortune in buying players for next to nothing and then selling them on for a fat profit. Bigger clubs, like Stoke and Aston Villa, had approached me to take over as manager, but I had always stayed loyal to Bournemouth.

Some may say that, as I left the club, I wasn't entitled to the remainder of my contract, but it wasn't quite like that. I outlined earlier in the book the disagreement I had with chairman Ken Gardiner, but there was more to my departure from Dean Court than that. A chap called Norman Hayward, later to take over as chairman, had also joined the club and he made it clear he wanted to play a big part in the running of Bournemouth and didn't want someone like me, who would be at his throat if ever he interfered in team matters, standing in his way. I think Hayward, no relation to Geoffrey Hayward who was to try to tempt me back to the club from West Ham a few years later, knew he'd have aggro with me. At the time the club also wanted to cut its wage bill and as I was getting £45,000 a year, or £65,000 when bonuses were included as was revealed in the local newspaper after I left, I think they felt they couldn't afford me. So I offered to go, but said that if I was on my bike, they'd better pay me what they owed me.

They got more from Harry Redknapp than Harry Redknapp got from Bournemouth, much as I loved the club. For years I kept Bournemouth going with my transfer dealings – for example Shaun Teale (bought for £50,000, sold for £500,000), Colin Clarke (bought for £20,000, sold for £500,000), and Ian Bishop, who I bought for £20,000 and sold for £750,000. They were massive deals for a club of Bournemouth's stature. But it didn't help that interest rates at the time were something like 15 per cent so the bank kept eating into whatever cash we had and we could never really get the overdraft down.

So I was disappointed that the Bournemouth fans reacted the way they did to what was called my golden handshake. They obviously thought I'd walked out on them to join West Ham and, like typical football fans, reckoned I wasn't entitled to another cent. But I could never hold any grudges towards them, or to Bournemouth itself. The club has a very special place in my heart and that was why I was willing to come to its rescue when it looked like going out of business a few seasons ago. I put a very substantial amount of money, an interest-free loan, into Bournemouth to keep it going. I'm not saying exactly how much but it was a very large sum. My accountant told me I was off my head – the odds are that I'll never get it back – but that's a measure of how much I care for the club. Trevor Watkins, the chairman, told me that the club was in deep trouble, that he needed to come up with a rescue package but was considerably short of what he required. He was resigned to the club going out of business. I didn't want to see Bournemouth die – it means too much to me and I have some very happy memories from my time there – and so I offered to help out.

It should also be remembered that I opted not to take a salary for about a four-month spell while I was manager in a bid to ease the club's cash plight. And if those cynical fans still believe I shouldn't have been paid that hundred grand, then I give you the name of Jamie Redknapp, signed for nothing and sold for £350,000, with another £350,000 eventually reaching the club after Jamie had made so many appearances for Liverpool. A man's entitled to £100,000 if a club gets £700,000 for his own kid!

It was a shame my time as Bournemouth manager ended in acrimony because I loved the nine years I spent there as boss. And remember it was with Bournemouth that I finished my playing career in the most memorable, for all the wrong reasons, of circumstances.

It was during the time I was assistant to Dave Webb at Dean Court that big-time soccer came calling again, with the most unfortunate of results. We were in the Fourth Division at the time and were given the plummiest of draws in the League Cup – a visit to Old Trafford to take on mighty Manchester United. Bryan Robson was on the pitch, so too Peter Beardsley in his only appearance for United, and on the opposition teamsheet, to the amusement of the few Bournemouth fans who'd made the trip north, appeared the name H Redknapp. We'd had a few injuries and out of the blue Webby asked me if I fancied playing. I hadn't trained seriously for ages, and hadn't played for even longer, and we were up against one of the best teams in the country. Did I fancy it? Too right I did. The old Redknapp skills were there. The pace had mostly gone, but I wasn't disgracing myself. I even found the time to chase back as United full back Ashley Grimes powered down the left wing. 'Come on Harry, get back, he's getting away from you. Quick Harry, he's going to cross, get your foot in. Quick, Quick. Oh no. What have I done?' As Grimes crossed, the ball cannoned off the outside of my foot and left our keeper, who'd come out to meet the cross, stranded as it looped into the net. We lost 2–0 and I realized there and then that it truly was time to bow out gracefully.

But I'd known a few years earlier that my best years as a player had long since passed. I'd flown back to England, after my first full season with Seattle Sounders, to look for a short-term contract with a club before the new campaign got started again Stateside. My knee injury had improved and I wasn't in a position to sit on my backside for those months. I had no money coming in and mouths to feed so when Brentford manager John Doherty called and invited me to join on a temporary basis, I was glad to accept. He gave me a run-out on my first Monday there in the reserves to sharpen me up for a first-team appearance the following Saturday. But at half-time John walked into the dressing room to announce he'd been sacked.

'I know I'm playing badly, John, but that's ridiculous,' I said. All the rest of the players fell about laughing but I don't think John saw the funny side of it. I was getting only £60 a week from Brentford and by the time I'd forked out for petrol driving up from my home in Bournemouth every day I was almost out of pocket. In my first game for the first team I broke three ribs after 25 minutes against Aldershot and knew things weren't going to work out. Quite simply, I couldn't afford to carry on playing for Brentford. I had Sandra and two young boys to look after and I wasn't earning any dough. One of my most vivid memories of that time was driving from home to training one winter morning in my battered Marina. The car wouldn't start for love nor money without a push, so poor Sandra, with two young kids around her ankles, would have to push me to the top of the hill where we lived. I'd look in my rear-view mirror and see a panting Sandra disappearing into the distance, the two boys chasing her, the dog chasing the two boys, and our two rabbits hopping around wondering what all the excitement was about.

People ask me whether I found it hard, after playing with World Cup footballers like Bobby Moore and Geoff Hurst, to cope with such a lower level of football, but I would argue all night that there were plenty of players in the lower divisions every bit as good as those in the top divisions. All they needed was the opportunity to show it. That argument is perhaps on shakier ground today with so many top-class foreigners flooding into our game, but a few years ago I could have named a squad of Second or Third Division players who could have held their own in the top flight. Look at those players who used to leave big clubs like Liverpool and West Ham and struggle. It was quite obvious they weren't much better than players in the bottom two divisions but had just been given the breaks.

When I first went to West Ham I bought a couple of lads from lower leagues who otherwise would never have got the chance and they did fantastically well for me. Players like Peter Butler and Matty Holmes. I bought Matty from Bournemouth for £40,000 and he ended up runner-up for Hammers player of the year. If I hadn't signed him, no way would he have been playing Premiership football. He later joined Blackburn in a deal worth £1.2million that saw Robbie Slater and £600,000 find their way to Upton Park. I was sorry to see Matty go. I remember when I was Bournemouth manager and I heard a thump,

thump, thump outside my office. The noise was driving me mad and when I looked out of the window it was a young kid booting a ball against the wall. I couldn't tell the kid to clear off – that wouldn't have been right – and I'm glad I didn't because it turned out it was Matty. I noticed him three weeks later at trials and he was outstanding. We signed him on YTS forms – and he carried on kicking the ball against my bloody wall. Matty plays football for the love of the game, not the money. Even when I told him of Blackburn's interest when he was at West Ham, even when he knew he could almost treble his wages, he wanted to stay at Upton Park because he was happy there. He's a throwback to the time when players loved the game. Now it's money, money, money. But it's time spent with people like Matt that gave me so much pleasure as a manager with limited funds.

I worked under several chairmen at Bournemouth – some I got on famously with, but others not so well. Rodney Barton was one chairman that I never really saw eye-to-eye with. Not long after I'd taken over as manager, Anton Johnson was replaced by Barton, who owned a company called Macbars. He was a big yachting man from the Isle Of Wight, very educated, very well-to-do. Rodney invited Sandra and I round to his house for his wife's birthday party. It was a Sunday and I wasn't really that keen on going as I wanted to spend the day at home with Sandra, but as it was the chairman I thought it politic to go. The party was full of yachties and yuppies and we felt uncomfortable. We walked into the kitchen to fetch a drink and saw Rodney's wife with her back to us talking to a friend.

'Oh my Simon's a wonderful football player,' her friend was saying. 'He's playing for the Second XI at public school. As your Rodney is manager of a football club, I wonder if he'd give him a trial.'

'Oh no,' Rodney's wife said. 'Rodney's not the manager. Heaven forbid, the manager's a nobody. Rodney's the chairman, if you don't mind.'

Before I could say or do anything, Sandra got hold of me and yanked me away. She knew what was coming.

I was proud of what I achieved as manager of Bournemouth. I was the longest-serving manager in the club's history, and I was the first to get them out of the old Third Division. They had a lot of top-class managers – Bill McGarry, Freddie Cox, John Bond – but it was me who took them to the dizzy heights of what is now the First Division but what of course was the Second Division then. We won the League in the 1986–87 season with 97 points with a team that cost me £50,000. I don't know the secret of that success. I was enthusiastic, maybe that rubbed off on the players, and I suppose I was lucky that the lads I got together formed a perfect blend. If there was a key player it was probably a big centre forward called Carl Richards. There lies a funny story. Richards had emerged from nowhere to star in non-League football for Enfield and had done so well that he'd forced his way into the England non-League squad. England were playing against Wales on an Easter Sunday at Nuneaton Borough and I knew it was my job to be there, much as Sandra moaned at me to stay at home. Richards impressed me with his pace and his strength and I thought I'd have a quiet word with him afterwards. When he walked into the bar afterwards, I couldn't believe it. What a specimen. He was well over 6ft and had muscles on muscles, an unbelievably powerful build.

'Oi, Oi,' I said, standing by the doorway and beckoning him with a backward nod. Very polished I was in those days. He looked at me as though I was something stupid. 'Hey, Carl,' I said. 'Can I have a word with you for a minute?' I had to be discreet because there were about half a dozen other League managers there on the prowl.

'Hello Carl,' I went on. 'I'm Harry Redknapp, manager of Bournemouth.'

'Yeah,' he said. 'What League are you in?'

'We're in the Third Division,' I said.

'Yeah, but what League?' he said. 'You're not in the Isthmian, are you?'

'No,' I said. 'Bournemouth. We're in the Football League.'

'I've never heard of you,' he said. Good start.

I signed Carl for £10,000 but he had a nightmare start. In training the first week he was there he couldn't do a thing, couldn't trap the ball, couldn't pass it, couldn't do anything. 'Oh no, what have I done?' I thought to myself. A week later Carl told me that his mate wanted a trial.

'Is he any good?' I asked.

'Not as good as me.'

'Well, I won't bother with him then', I answered. A few weeks later we were playing Crystal Palace in a pre-season friendly and Carl told me his mate, the same guy I'd ignored, had impressed Palace in a trial and was due to face us that day. No worries there, I thought. But this guy was different class. Afterwards I said to Carl: 'I thought you said he wasn't as good as you. Are you sure?'

The guy's name? Ian Wright. Well I missed out on him then but I've got him now!

Carl turned out to be a massive success for us. Opposing defences couldn't handle him. But off the field he didn't have a clue. The first week he got paid he came to my office and accused me of fiddling him.

'You told me I'd be getting £250 a week but I'm only getting £190,' he complained.

'That's your tax and stuff,' I said.

He looked at me accusingly. 'You didn't tell me anything about this.'

'That's your income tax,' I said, amazed. 'Everyone in the country has to pay it. When you went to work before you joined us you must have paid tax, didn't you?'

'I've never been to work,' he said. He was 26 and had never had a job in his life.

'At Enfield they said they'd give me £80 a week and that's

what they gave me, £80 a week,' he went on. 'I want £250 here.'

So every week he'd come into my office to complain about his wages. He had a girlfriend and little baby and wanted to buy a house. 'What do I do?' he asked me.

A day later he came into my office, said he'd done what I told him, and that he'd bought a house for £37,500. 'Really, after just one day?' I asked. 'What's it like?"

'Three bathrooms and one bedroom,' he said.

'Don't you mean *three* bedrooms and *one* bathroom?'

'Oh, something like that,' he said.

It turned out he'd looked in the estate agents' window and bought the first house he'd seen, without even going to look at it. I rang the estate agents and told them that there'd been a mistake, that Carl couldn't afford more than £35,000, and they were so desperate for the sale they flogged it to him for that.

He had a great first season for us, forming a great combination with Trevor Aylott which swept us to the Third Division title, but he found life in the higher division much tougher and his form suffered. We were at home to Birmingham one day and their chairman Ken Wheldon approached me. 'Your boy Richards,' he said to me. 'We'll give you £70,000 for him.' I couldn't believe my luck but had to play it cool. 'Well to be honest we're looking for a bit more for him,' I said.

'All right,' he said. 'But I don't want any messing about. I'll give you £75,000, and that's my final offer.'

And off he went to Birmingham where he struggled to make an impact.

Bournemouth was a great grounding for me as a manager. Unlike some young bosses coming into the game with no background in coaching or management, I had to serve my apprenticeship. And it was tough. We had no training ground so it was a daily chore to find somewhere to train on a parks pitch, ordering the kids out first with a broom and a shovel to clear up all the dog mess. After training we'd spend an hour looking for lost balls. Each one lost was a minor catastrophe. We didn't have laundry or changes of kit. The players had to take their gear home each day and wash it. That's why I like loaning players out to lower-division clubs. It's the greatest education they can have. Rio Ferdinand went on loan to Bournemouth , Frank Lampard to Swansea, and I think it was the making of them. They suddenly realized how lucky they were. They have a woman that cooks lunches for them, enjoy a lovely changing room, a cup of tea when they finish training, sauna in the dressing room, it's a different world. Then they go down to Swansea, probably have to drive to a windswept training ground, and are lucky even to get a cuppa afterwards.

Even when we beat Manchester United in the FA Cup in 1984 and the whole town was alive, I was quickly brought down to earth with a bump. We trained the following Monday on an artificial pitch owned by the council. We weren't supposed to use it but the gate was open, there was no one around so we thought we might as well. When we finished we found the groundsman had locked us in and bolted the gate. That was Bournemouth for you. On Saturday night we'd been on *Match Of The Day* and were the toast of the country; on the Monday this geezer has ridden up on his bike, thought 'I'll show them,' and locked us in. These young boys at West Ham, in fact young players who have gone straight to any Premiership club, don't know they're born.

But I loved it. It was my first job and I was so excited. And things went really well for me. The team enjoyed success, and I was very popular with the fans. As I said I was the first manager to take the club into the Second Division (the First Division now) and, without making excuses, we could have stayed there but for a disastrous run of injuries that decimated my squad. My whole life revolved around watching football. I became a walking encyclopaedia of lower-division and non-League players. It was common for me to drive four hours to watch a midweek match, only for me to discover on arrival that the player I'd gone to watch wasn't even playing. I watched a million matches, but I loved it all. If there was a game I was there, always on the look-out for a bargain.

Of course all this must have been hard on Sandra. I was never at home. But she knew that this was my big chance, that if I could make a success of this then we'd be set up okay. Up until then it had been a struggle for us. We'd enjoyed a decent lifestyle in America but we'd never put any money away, and when we returned I was earning next to nothing at Oxford City alongside Bobby Moore. Towards the end of my playing career I had found myself training with Brentford, driving a clapped-out Morris Marina with Sandra, giving me a push start in the morning. Behind me then, and behind me fully in those early days at Bournemouth. I was to need her love and support even more a few years later, in the summer of 1990.

CHAPTER 6

Death in Italy

For every football fan a World Cup year normally means a summer of golden memories, but the feast of international football we enjoy every four years is a painful reminder of the saddest chapter of my life.

Italia '90. Even now that simple phrase makes me shudder. Italia '90. For most people it evokes memories of Gazza's tears, England's heroic near-miss, Pavarotti and *Nessun Dorma*. But for me there is no such golden nostalgia. For Italia '90 claimed the life of my very good friend Brian Tiler, and so nearly booked me a date with my maker.

There was no hint of the horrors to come when I woke that blisteringly hot day in Rome. I felt like I was in paradise, but the beautiful dream was soon to turn into the worst kind of nightmare. I was Bournemouth manager at the time and had gone with Brian and some other mates – Michael Sinclair, who at the time was chairman of York City, and Eric Whitehouse, who was a big Aston Villa supporter, and their boys – to watch a few games. We had tickets for a lot of the opening group matches, plus a couple of quarter-finals, the semi-final and final. Clearly it was a holiday, as there was no way Bournemouth could afford to buy any of the players on view in the World Cup no matter how desperately I'd have tried.

Our hotel, a real beauty, was right on the coast. We sat round the pool during the day, relaxing in the sun, and having a laugh. The pressures of the season were a million miles away. It was paradise. We had hired a mini-bus and driver to take us to and from games, and on this particular day, 30 June, were looking forward to watching Italy, the host nation with Roberto Baggio in sparkling form, take on the Republic of Ireland. Bournemouth keeper Gerry Peyton was in the Irish squad, although only as reserve to first-choice Paki Bonner. We watched the game, in which Ireland performed brilliantly only to lose to a goal from Toto Schillaci, who if I remember rightly finished top scorer in that tournament. Not that I have much recollection of what happened afterwards.

Following the game we bumped into a few friends from Bournemouth in a little restaurant around the corner from the ground. There were loads of Irish fans there and they got talking about Gerry Peyton. We were having a good crack. As the evening wore on the rest of my group were on the bus waiting to get back to our hotel, but I kept them hanging around for about 10 minutes talking to these Irish lads. Maybe if I hadn't done that we'd have got home in one piece. Maybe if I hadn't done that Brian Tiler would be here today. The next day England were due to take on the Cameroons and we had mapped out our schedule for that one. But we were never to make it to the ground.

In the minibus on the way back to the hotel most of us were either asleep or dozing. That's as much as I can remember. Then, at around midnight, in a place called Latina, just south of Rome, I'm told a car hurtled towards us on the wrong side of the road. I'm told it was going 90 miles an hour. I'm told the smash was so horrific that it was a miracle anyone got out alive. Brian didn't. Nor did the occupants of the other car, three Italian lads who all died instantly. The force of the impact threw me out of the minibus and knocked me unconscious. I was then dragged away from the mangled wreckage, covered in petrol, by Michael Sinclair, who was petrified by the thought that it would all explode. To my knowledge it was never confirmed if the Italian lads were drunk or not, but apparently they'd spent all day at the beach before watching the Italy-Ireland game on TV, and the fact they were going 90 miles an hour on the wrong side of the road offers a few clues.

The first thing I remember was waking up in hospital two days later, unaware of the extent of my injuries, and unaware that Brian had died. The emergency services at the scene of the crash had apparently thought I was a goner and pulled a blanket over my head. Even my watch had gone, someone clearly believing I wouldn't be needing it. Everything of value had gone. The doctors, I'm told, also thought I was dead upon arrival at the hospital. But I was lucky. I had fractured my skull, broken several bones, and suffered a horrific gash to my leg, but I don't think the injuries, though serious, were ever life-threatening, despite those first impressions. Looking later at pictures of the wreckage I can't believe we all weren't killed. The mini-bus was completely wiped out. The driver, an Italian, spent nine months in hospital. But the injuries to the rest of the passengers were not too serious.

People ask me how Brian was the only passenger who didn't survive the accident. Was it the seating arrangements, seat belts, or pure bad luck? I have to say I cannot give an answer. The whole thing is still a blur. I can remember virtually nothing, apart from the fact that I was sitting alongside Brian – me on the aisle seat, Brian next to the window.

I wasn't told of Brian's death until long after I regained consciousness. I couldn't believe it. My mate. We had gone through so much together and shared so many laughs. Gone.

Just like that. How must his wife Hazel and daughter Michelle be feeling? I miss Brian so much. He was a massive part of my life. I had a fantastic relationship at Bournemouth with him. He was a terrific feller to work with. He knew my moods better than anyone. He knew when I was down and every now and again if I had the hump with someone, or had had a row with the chairman, he'd whisk me off to Ascot races for the day. A really wonderful bloke. We hit it off from day one and never had a cross word. He never interfered in anything I did at Bournemouth, always backing my managerial decisions, and if ever any of the directors at a board meeting criticized me, he would jump in to defend me. To think that he is no longer here is deeply saddening, but I still have the comfort of some wonderful memories.

I remember the day I signed my last contract at Bournemouth, in January 1989, and we were in Hull preparing for a match. In all the time I've been in football I've never had a real drink on the Friday. I'm not a big boozer. I enjoy a drink socially, but I don't drink beer. I stick to wine with a meal, or maybe the odd glass of champagne, but I must have made up for years of abstinence that night. It was late in the season and there was nothing to play for in the following day's match, so Brian suggested we go out and celebrate my new three-year contract. I was all for it. I'd never made any money out of football, like most of the players of my generation, but for the first time this contract was going to guarantee me a nice living. So I was in the mood to celebrate. We went to a Chinese restaurant in Hull and started off with a couple of Bacardi and Cokes each. We then got through three bottles of red wine, a couple of brandies, and a bottle of champagne. By this stage, needless to say, we were rather the worse for wear. Brian and I kidded the manager of the restaurant that we had a hot tip on the horses the next day but wouldn't find out the name until the morning so he was all over us. He even drove us back to our hotel to make sure we wouldn't forget to phone him. When we got back Brian insisted on another bottle of champagne. I'm not kidding you, when I stumbled back to my room I must have bounced off every wall in the corridor.

The next day I was out of it. I just couldn't recover. I'd never been so ill in my whole life, but Brian was right as rain, as though he'd gone to bed at 9pm the night before. The players knew there was something wrong with me but never guessed it was almost a case of alcoholic poisoning because they knew I wasn't a big drinker. At half-time we were 4–0 down. I walked into the dressing room and all I could say was: 'Come on lads, we've got to do better than this,' before walking out again. They must have looked at me as if I was from another planet. My head was exploding.

But that's how Brian was. Great company. Great feller. I miss him.

I spent three weeks in hospital in Latina, but it was a bit of a dump and my family who had gone out to Italy to be with me wanted me home. A firm called Euro-Assist, which has special low-flying jets – I couldn't be flown home by normal aircraft because of the fractures to my skull – flew me right into Hurn Airport in Bournemouth. The flight cost about £10,000, which the club very kindly paid for. After returning to England my recovery period was slow. I knew I'd get back to my career as Bournemouth manager, the only question was when. I was under doctor's orders not to go to any games. I was told by a lawyer that if I didn't return to work for 18 months I'd be in line for a massive insurance pay-out, but that was never an option. I just wanted to get back to work. Doing nothing would have driven me around the bend. The money wasn't important. Still isn't. I could *afford* to live without football, but I couldn't actually *live* without football.

I missed the game so much that I remember going to watch a Bournemouth match at Aldershot incognito. I hid at the back of the stand with a baseball cap on, sunglasses, coat pulled up around my neck. It was real cloak-and-dagger stuff. The doctor looking after me would have gone crazy if he'd known.

When I look back on the accident now, it hasn't altered my outlook on life although I suppose for a while it put things into perspective. I thought at the time that there was no way I'd allow football to be the be-all and end-all of life for me, that I would in future be able to switch off. But within a few months I was just like I'd always been. Still getting the hump when we got beat, and taking everything too personally. I'd be lying if I said it radically changed my life. For a while I completely lost my sense of taste and smell. I wouldn't have a clue what I was eating. The taste came back, though not fully, after about six months but even today I can't smell anything. You could put a jar of mint sauce and Julian Dicks' smelly socks beneath my nose but if I had my eyes closed I couldn't tell which was which. But it's probably an advantage as I spend so much time in a dressing room with some of my West Ham players!

But that terrible accident, apart from the heartbreak of Brian's death and the worry it caused my loved ones, was to haunt me further still. First there was the incident I've already described involving Bournemouth chairman Ken Gardiner. Then, after I'd become Billy Bonds' assistant at West Ham, a sickening comment from a Bristol City fan sparked a reaction that almost got me into very hot water.

Before I recount it, I should admit here that I've been critical many times about the behaviour of supporters. Not all of course. Where would football be without them? I'm talking about the small minority who enjoy causing trouble, who think it's their right to hurl personal abuse at players and managers but who demand action if similar abuse is turned on them. I remember back in 1990, shortly before that car crash in Italy, Bournemouth played Leeds at our Dean Court ground on a Bank Holiday weekend. It was a crucial fixture which saw us get relegated and Leeds go up as Second Division champions. But the impact of the result was at the time of secondary importance because the match was scarred by scenes of sickening violence by Leeds fans. I think police made almost 100 arrests and 20 fans were badly injured. Five police officers were also hurt, two seriously. I called for Leeds United to condemn their travelling fans, and I remember that the language I used caused quite a stir in the newspapers.

'It's about time Leeds came out and said: "You are scum. We don't want you,"' I was reported as saying at the time. But I really did feel so strongly. I had never seen scenes of such mindless violence in all my years in football. I was so concerned for the safety of our supporters that it was impossible to concentrate on the game. But I had suspected a week earlier that the game would not pass peacefully. We were at Sheffield United on the same day Leeds were at home. Leeds drew, a bad result considering they had a team containing the likes of Gordon Strachan and Gary Speed, real top-drawer players, while we lost at Sheffield. On the motorway on the way back we were surrounded by cars and vans full of Leeds fans. They were making vile gestures towards us, slowing us up to about 10 miles an hour, sticking their arses out of the window. It was clear the following weekend's clash at Dean Court would not be without incident.

Thousands of Leeds fans came down to Bournemouth on the Friday night and wrecked the town. There must have been about 15,000 fans at the ground, the next morning, most of them desperately trying to get tickets for the game. Bournemouth is a very quite place, there's never any aggro and the fans are not your normal football supporters. They're a different breed. Bournemouth fans were coming to the game and having their tickets taken off them by these rampaging Leeds fans. They just ran riot. Every car in the car park was smashed to pieces. Things were so bad that the local police were running away from Leeds supporters. They took the whole ground over. There was hardly a Bournemouth supporter in the place, and those that were there were too frightened to open their mouths. It made you sad for football.

A year earlier I'd taken criticism for my views on fencing at football grounds in the wake of the Hillsborough disaster. I was quoted at length in a back-page story in the local paper, the Bournemouth *Daily Echo*. 'Do you think that because of Hillsborough the hooligans who caused us to put barriers up in the first place are suddenly going to behave?' I said. 'Of course they are not. The blame for the tragedy lies ultimately at their door because it is their idiocy that made the fences necessary in the first place. We would never have had them if it wasn't for the nutters. I was at the Chelsea–Middlesbrough play-off game last season and I witnessed unbelievable violence. If the fences hadn't been there the Chelsea fans would have charged into the visitors' enclosure and there would have been murder on the pitch. It would have been carnage. People must not forget the nutters are still around and we do not want them getting at people at our stadium if they come to watch a game in Bournemouth. The fences, however much we hate them, must remain.'

I suppose at the time it was a controversial view and I must admit that it has changed over the years. I don't want to see fences, but at the same time how are we going to stop these nutters? Look at those incidents towards the end of the 1997–98 season when Liverpool's Paul Ince and Barnsley's Jan-Aage Fjortoft had to wrestle with supporters who had invaded the pitch. And what about that incident when the linesman was punched by a madman at Portsmouth? He should be put away for a couple of years to set an example. If people think they can get away with punching a linesman, what next? A referee being stabbed? I don't want to see people being fenced in like animals – the horrific images of Hillsborough are impossible to forget; I just want to see people behaving themselves.

I mention all this to give you an insight into my feelings the night of 15 September 1992, a month after joining Hammers as assistant boss, when I was accused of sparking a mini-riot. We were at Bristol City, playing really well, and leading 3–1. All night we were getting abuse from the City fans. Crazy they are there, absolutely wild. Alvin Martin went down injured in the second half. I was on the pitch making sure Alvin was okay and as I walked back to the dug-out one of their supporters snarled: 'You should have f****** been killed in Italy with your f****** mate.' I ask you. What kind of person says a vile thing like that over a football match? I reacted, anyone would, and was charged with making a V-sign to the fan. But I swear I didn't. Honest to God I put three fingers up on one hand and one finger on the other to signal the score, smiled at him, and then sat down. But minutes later a fight broke out in the stand immediately behind the dug-out. A steward standing some 40 yards away rushed over and said he saw me making an obscene gesture. I was flabbergasted.

After the game there was a knock on the dressing-room door and in walked two coppers wanting to interview me. They said they were going to report me for inciting the crowd. It could have turned very nasty for me, with the FA threatening to take action, but for a stroke of luck. Behind the dug-out there was a schoolteacher, a doctor, and several other responsible people who wrote to West Ham to support me. They said they'd seen everything and that I hadn't put two fingers up to the crowd. As if I would have done anyway. I'm not that silly.

CHAPTER 7

The Chips and Lager Diet

There is no greater pleasure in football as a coach than seeing a move you've worked on all week in training pay rich dividends on a Saturday. It's sheer bliss. We all remember the stunning goal from a free kick Argentina scored against England in the World Cup in France in 1998 and it's hard to recall a more perfectly worked goal. I shudder to think how much time Daniel Passarella, the Argentine coach, spent with his players in training fine-tuning that move. At West Ham earlier that season we so nearly pulled a similar stroke only for Samassi Abou to miss an open goal and ruin all the hard work. Eyal Berkovic stood over a free kick 10 yards from the box but then suddenly began to walk away. Young Frank Lampard stepped up and played the ball short for Stan Lazaridis, who had lined up on the edge of the defensive wall but then spun off behind it just before Frank played the pass. Stan was then in the clear but when he squared it across goal Abou missed an absolute sitter to wreck what would have been a picturebook goal. So much for all the work in training.

Any training session has to start with stretching exercises. That is absolutely crucial. Arsene Wenger at Arsenal is a big advocate of that and look how well it's worked for the Gunners. After a brief warm-up I'll get the players working in little groups, two on two, three on three, that kind of thing. It's always competitive and benefits both the forwards and defenders. I like getting the first team in full-scale practice matches to work on things we might try on a Saturday, working the ball to the front two, getting them to link up, maybe one letting the ball run to the other and then spinning off. We also work on corners and try to perfect what we call 'the block'. A forward will run towards the corner kicker and take his marker with him before turning and running the other way, the idea being that he then gets himself between a team-mate and that team-mate's marker, leaving his colleague in theory with a free header.

It's no secret in football circles that I'm highly regarded as a coach. Jimmy Gabriel saw enough in me at Bournemouth to whisk me off to the States, Bobby Moore always wanted me to work alongside him, and there's no way I'd have had the success I enjoyed on limited resources at Bournemouth without knowing a thing or two about coaching. I've tried to ally all the things I have learned over the years from people like Ron Greenwood and John Bond to a natural in-built enthusiasm for the game. You could be the greatest tactician in the world but if you can't spark the players then you're no use to anyone. If a coach turns up for training with little or no enthusiasm, then how can he expect his players to have any?

Ron Greenwood had a big influence on me. He was West Ham manager when I arrived at Upton Park in 1963 and he was a fantastic coach. Every day in training was different, he could see things in a game that no one else could. He was miles ahead of anyone. I remember going to Lilleshall with the England youth side as a 16-year-old and during a practice game the ball was played to me about 10 yards from the touchline. I held the ball up and screamed for the full back to come outside me. The coach asked me what I was trying to do and I told him I wanted him to go on the overlap. Well, he looked at me as if I was from a different planet, didn't have a clue what I was going on about. But that night he and the rest of the coaches at Lilleshall spent hours talking about this overlapping tactic and they all loved it. But we'd been doing that at West Ham for ages. I know this sounds silly now but back in those early Sixties there was no such thing as overlapping full backs. That's how Ron was. He had so many new ideas.

But I think Ron had it tough handling the West Ham lads in those days. When you look at the players at Upton Park at that time we didn't achieve half of what we were capable of. Speaking as a manager now, there's no way I would stand for some of the things Ron had to tolerate. Come 5.30pm on a Saturday after home games, every West Ham player would be in the Black Lion pub in Plaistow, and on the train coming back from away games half a dozen or so players would knock back lager like you've never seen. We would play cards en route to an away game on a Friday, go to the dogs that night, and then get back to the hotel and resume the card school until the early hours of the morning. Sometimes the match the next day interrupted the card game. There's no way that could happen today. I know I'm known as a gambler but I will not allow serious card schools to develop at West Ham. It doesn't do you any good as a footballer, or much for your mental state on the pitch, to lose £2,000 before a game. During my playing days, on occasions I lost up to £200 in high-stakes card games at a time when I was earning £40 a week and it did my brain in. There was obviously a lack of discipline there somewhere but Ron should not take the blame. He couldn't be with us every minute of the day. There had to be some self-discipline too. Looking back we got away with murder.

Towards the end of my playing career, in 1972, I joined

Bournemouth where John Bond, a former Hammers player, was manager. John was also a great coach, full of ideas. He'd learned a lot from Ron Greenwood too, but he was very much his own man, very flamboyant. He also liked to hear himself talk. At one club he was at the players used to run a book on how long his team meetings would last, but he talked a lot of sense. And he always put a lot of thought into training sessions. His assistant was Kenny Brown, who'd had a wonderful career with West Ham and played for England, and they made a good team. While Bondy would play the bad cop, giving players stick, Kenny would butter them up, having a laugh and a joke.

I was staying in digs on a Friday night before my first game for Bournemouth and I was feeling bored. Suddenly I got an idea. There used to be a reporter for the *Sunday People* called Sam Bartram who from time to time rang me for titbits – team news, transfers and the like – and send me the odd tenner for my trouble. I thought I'd pretend to be Sam and ring up Bill Kitchener, one of the Bournemouth players who used to be a West Ham team-mate.

'Hello, is Bill there?' I asked his wife Dawn.

'No, he's just popped out. Who's speaking?'

'It's Sam Bartram here. *Sunday People*. I'm just doing a piece for Sunday's paper about the new season and I thought I'd get Bill's thoughts. There's a fee involved. Fifty quid.'

'Ooh, he won't be long,' she said, suddenly now anxious. 'Could you ring back in 10 minutes?'

'No, sorry love. I'm on a deadline. I've another name here to ring. Mel Machin. I think I'll try him.'

'No don't ring him,' she said. 'He gets everything. Bill will be back soon.'

But I rang Mel, who I'd only known a week in training, and gave him the same spiel about wanting someone on the inside to feed me details about Bournemouth. I told him there was £50 up front, with a further £25 guaranteed every week.

'Oh lovely, Sam,' he said. 'I'm in a card school with Bondy

and he always tells us what's going on so I should be able to get you loads of information. In fact he's interested in Bobby Kellard at the moment at Portsmouth.'

'That's great, Mel,' I said. 'That's a lovely one to start with. And how about that Harry Redknapp? How's he settling in at Bournemouth? I hear he's a bit of a lad.'

'Yeah, he's great is Harry. I'm really looking forward to playing with him.'

'That's lovely,' I said. 'Okay Mel, there's a cheque for £50 in the post and I'll speak to you next week.'

The next day at the pre-match meal Mel was sitting next to Ted MacDougall who was telling him about all the deals he had with newspapers and magazines – £40 for *Shoot*, £30 for *Match*, plus dozens of others. Mel couldn't wait to tell him about the *Sunday People* deal, and then pointed at the brand new suit he was wearing. 'Look at this, Ted,' he said. 'Just got it run up for me at the tailor's. Sixty quid it set me back, but there's 50 quid on the way for me from the *Sunday People*.'

I could hardly keep my face straight by now. In the dressing room before the game Mel was still bubbling about his new sideline. 'Alright Sam?' I said to him.

He look at me a little puzzled and nodded back. 'Okay Harry.'

A couple of minutes later I said to him. 'Looking forward to the game Sam?'

'What are you calling me Sam for?' he asked.

'Well you're Sam Bartram aren't you?'

'How did you know?' he said, quickly looking in every direction to make sure no one could hear. 'Don't tell anyone.'

'No problem, Sam,' I said, continuing the wind-up. 'So I hear Bobby Kellard's coming.'

Mel's face was a picture. 'Who told you?' he gasped.

'*I'm* Sam Bartram,' I said.

'What are you going on about?' Mel asked.

'I am Sam, Sam Bartram,' I repeated.

Just then it dawned on Mel that he'd been done up like a kipper. He went spare, but when Bondy heard about it he beamed like a Cheshire cat.

'I love it, I love it,' he said. 'This feller's gonna slaughter you lot,' he told the rest of the Bournemouth players. 'You won't be able to live with Harry.'

That was an hour before the game, but five minutes after the game, and following a scrappy performance from Bournemouth, he'd changed his tune. He went through each player one by one, dishing out stick, and when he got to me he said:

'...And you. If you think you're coming down here merely to take the piss you can piss off now.' And that was Bondy in a nutshell. But he had a lot to offer. He had a great personality, he was fun to be with, and he could get a lot out of his players. He was a good coach and I enjoyed working with him.

Bondy signed a player called Alan Groves from Shrewsbury Town. Alan had come into the game late after spending years as a long-distance lorry driver and playing only part-time football. This boy could have been one of the greatest players ever. He was a great big lad, a left-winger, with skill, strength and pace like no other player I've seen in my life. We played against him while he was with Shrewsbury and he absolutely slaughtered us on his own. So Bondy shelled out £50,000 for him. What a character he was. Always happy, always laughing. The only problem with him was that he was my room-mate and he smoked 70 fags a day. But run! You've never seen anyone so fast. In a 20-yard sprint he could hop the last 10 yards and still leave the rest of us standing. How he didn't go right to the top I'll never know. After a couple of weeks at Bournemouth Alan bought himself an E-type Jag, with one of those silly horns that you still hear on some teenagers' cars now. This new car pleased Bondy no end. In a team meeting he said he wanted all of us to drive E-type Jags or Mercedes.

'I don't want to see Morris Marinas or minis out there. I want to see Jags like Grovesie's got. Show a bit of class.'

The thing was, Bondy had heard Brian Clough give the same opinion on telly the week before and thought it sounded good, but after three weeks we hadn't won a game and Bondy once again turned full circle.

'And you Groves, if you think you're going to be driving round the town showing off in that f****** Jag all day and blowing that stupid 'ooter, you'll be on your bike. If I ever see that car in the car park again you're going. Sell it.'

'But boss,' Grovesie began.

'I'm telling you now,' Bondy cut in, 'either the car goes or you go.'

I think a lot of Bondy's techniques were honed while he was a player at West Ham and he would join the Hammers 'think tank' in the café around the corner from the ground. Bondy, Noel Cantwell, Malcolm Allison, Frank O'Farrell, Jimmy Andrews, Ernie Gregory and Dave Sexton would all sit there talking about football. Allison was the guv'nor and he'd be moving the salt and pepper pots around to demonstrate his tactics. That was a hotbed of coaching talent because they all went on to become successful managers.

For a perfect illustration of Bondy's talents you have only to look at the progress he made with his son Kevin. John signed Kevin while he was at Bournemouth and if ever there was a player you could be confident would not make the grade it was him. He was like Bambi on ice. All legs, no strength. He didn't even play for the school team, never mind a district side. We all thought it was a touch of nepotism on Bondy's part, signing his own son – maybe I was to be guilty of that later on but I'd have to say there was a world of difference between Kevin Bond and Jamie Redknapp as teenagers – but he obviously saw something in Kevin that no one else could. If we did a two-lap warm-up Kevin would be half a lap behind the rest of us. Not one single person apart from John thought his son would ever make a player. But he improved out of recognition, and went on to be player of the year at Manchester City and Southampton, and proved a fantastic signing for me when I was manager at Bournemouth. Kevin's now No 2 to Alan Ball at Portsmouth and I think he's got a big future in the game.

But it's not always coaching that brings out the best in a player. Sometimes self-determination and a belief in your own ability can be the most effective trump cards. Look at Frank Lampard, my assistant at West Ham. Frank was a good schoolboy player without being special, but he knuckled down better than anyone I've ever seen to make it to the very top. He is the perfect example to young players. I remember Ron Greenwood coming into the Hammers dressing room one day when Frank was about 17 years old and telling him that Torquay wanted him on loan. If they like you, Ron told him, we'll make it a permanent signing.

Frank was bewildered. 'What do I want to go to Torquay for?' he said. 'I play for West Ham.' That was a measure of Frank's bottle. Most kids his age in the same situation would have taken it on the chin. 'What's wrong with me?' Frank went on. 'You've never said anything was wrong.'

This put Ron on the spot. He had to tell Frank honestly what he thought. 'Well you're short of pace,' he said. 'You're not going to be quick enough to make it. And your passing's not up to it.'

Some players may have been crushed but Frank is made of sterner stuff. 'I'll show you,' he said. And after that he would come back for an extra session of training every day of every week, Sundays included. He would do an hour of sprints, five yards one way and then turning for a five-yard sprint the opposite way. He'd spend an hour and a half chipping balls to get his passing right, and then he'd rope someone in to try to take the ball past him. This was every single day. From being slow he got quicker and quicker. His passing improved and with it his all-round game, so much so that he went on to be capped for England. Frank certainly had something about him. Peter Brabrook, an England international, arrived at West Ham when Frank was a mere 17-year-old. Peter could do tricks with the ball you'd never believe, dancing around it and sending his opponent every which way. One day in training he was working on some flashy moves when Frank landed an almighty kick across Peter's knees and the established international understandably got angry. 'What are you doing, kicking me?' he shouted at Frank. 'Try to take the piss out of me,' Frank answered, 'and I'll kick you even harder next time.'

One of the most frustrating aspects of being a coach is to regularly see players perform brilliantly in training only for them to fail to reproduce that form on the Saturday. I paid £70,000 to take a boy called Shaun Close from Spurs to Bournemouth and in training he looked a world-beater. But somehow he lacked the confidence to translate that obvious ability into the real thing during a match. There have been hundreds of opposite examples – players who perform with two left feet in training only to improve 100 per cent on match-day. Some centre backs for instance will not be at their best in five-a-sides – their strengths are tackling and heading and stopping players – but come Saturday they turn it on and that's where it counts.

I will explain later why Florin Raducioiu and Marco Boogers were my worst signings as a manager, but there are a number of candidates for my best buy. Shaun Teale, who went on to play so brilliantly for Aston Villa a few years back, was one of them. I saw Teale play for non-League Weymouth a few times and I was desperate to sign him for Bournemouth. I thought he was a terrific player. The Weymouth manager was Stuart Morgan, who was a good pal of mine, and I'd told him that we were willing to give £50,000. I also told Stuart that if he could sell at that figure, there'd be a job for him working alongside me at Bournemouth. But before any deal could be struck,

Stuart got a call from Reading saying they would pay £100,000 for Teale.

'Harry, what am I going to do?' Stuart asked.

'Well if I don't get Teale, you ain't got a job with me, have you?' I said.

Reading were due to approach Teale that day, but Stuart fixed up a meeting with me first and we got him for £50,000, with Stuart later joining me at Bournemouth. Weymouth won't be too happy when they read this, but that's football. Teale gave us three years of great service and we sold him on for £500,000 to Aston Villa.

I think the player who most impressed me for his professionalism, and proved a great signing for me at Bournemouth, was Luther Blissett, who played for England but who found it hard to recover from an unfortunate spell in Italy when he was re-christened Luther 'Mis-hit'. I paid Watford £40,000 for Luther, in November 1988, and it was perhaps the best 40 grand I've ever spent. He had a massive influence on all the young players at the club although not on the local media! I remember him sitting in the stands watching one of our games just after he'd signed. One of the local newspaper reporters must have thought he'd recognized him and went up for a few words.

'What are you doing in Bournemouth?' the reporter asked Luther. 'Are you *appearing* here?' Luther looked at him, puzzled. It turned out he'd been mistaken for Kenny Lynch!

In truth I ran into a little opposition from the Bournemouth vice-chairman Peter Hayward after I'd signed Blissett. 'He's over the hill. He's had his day,' Hayward said. That night we were at home to Hull. By half-time we were 4–0 up, all four scored by Blissett on his debut. 'We haven't seen the best of him yet,' Hayward was then telling everyone who wanted to listen. 'Are you sure?' I asked him. 'Four goals in one half – it doesn't get much better than that.'

Luther looked after himself incredibly well. He was the first professional footballer I'd come across who followed a strict diet, eating pasta, drinking only water, the kind of thing everyone takes for granted nowadays. Luther picked up all those good habits in Italy. Suddenly all the Bournemouth players followed suit. That was great news for me because I owned the local Italian restaurant, Lorenzo's, and every day all the players would be in there eating their pasta. So Luther was the top man for me.

As someone who earned a living playing football in the 1960s, when players thought nothing about diets and were only too ready to spend all day boozing, I was perhaps slow to recognize how important the right food and the right preparation is to a professional athlete. Don't get me wrong, if you can't play, no diet on earth is going to help you, no matter how healthy or beneficial. But I understand now as a coach how crucial such things are if you're going to stay at the top of your profession. It's no good saying we won the World Cup on a diet of chips and lager. Football the world over has improved massively, and taken unbelievable steps forward, but the game in Britain has not kept pace. Players used to sit in the pub and arrogantly proclaim that their Italian counterparts were obliged to eat all the right food, stay off the booze, and live like monks because of the massive money they earned. But that's no longer applicable as players in Britain are earning fortunes now. If you're earning 10 grand a week, you're obliged not to be out on the booze; you're obliged to eat the right food, look after yourself. In the old days footballers earned only slightly more than the average man in the street; now they are on a hundred times more so it should be no sacrifice to temper their lifestyles. And there's no doubt in my mind that the right diet and preparation improves a player's performance. Today's players are more supple, have more energy, are perhaps even more alert.

I read a story during the World Cup in the summer of 1998 that some England players were prescribed what was described as a wonder pill in France. It's something called creatine and by all accounts improved fitness levels incredibly. There's nothing illegal about the pill, and I know for a fact Arsene Wenger used it at Arsenal during the 1997–98 season and look what happened to them. Arsenal centre half Steve Bould reckons he's had four years added to his career by Wenger's arrival. He told John Hartson a couple of years ago that he didn't think he had another run left in him, but with a different diet, different training methods, different preparation, he now feels he can go on another two years. I'm sure many other clubs will follow Wenger's examples. I know that creatine is frowned upon in some quarters with people worrying about its long-term effect, but I'm sure top doctors would not be recommending it if it was harmful. It's certainly something I shall seriously consider using at West Ham.

As a coach it's vitally important to develop your youth set-up, particularly at a club like West Ham which is never going to compete with the likes of Manchester United, Liverpool, and Arsenal for the real star signings. When I was a kid Ron Greenwood would come and watch all the youth games at West Ham and that made us feel important, and it's something I've taken on. Frank and I attend as many youth games as we can, checking out the kids on a Saturday morning before joining up with the first team later on. I've had to make some tough decisions at West Ham to radically alter our youth policy. In the Sixties the club prided itself on attracting all the best youngsters from the area, but up until recently we hadn't produced a top local player for something like 10 years. Players who should have graduated at West Ham – top talent like Tony Adams, David Beckham, Ray Parlour, and Sol Campbell – had escaped the net and I had to do something about it. That meant upsetting people who had been at the club a long time, good friends among them, but I had to shake things up. It wasn't easy, believe me. Ronnie Boyce had been a fantastic servant to the club and someone I like a lot, but I had to let him go when

I changed the scouting system. I just thought things had gone a bit stale. But it's ultimately the manager who carries the can. You can keep good friends at the club if you want but you're the one who gets the sack if things go wrong. As a manager you must employ the people you think can do the best job for you and that often means making tough decisions. I brought in Jimmy Hampson from Charlton as youth development officer, with Tony Carr and Peter Brabrook also fulfilling valuable roles. During the 1997–98 season I had Frank Burrows, who has been around for years and has been a manager in his own right at clubs like Portsmouth, Swansea and Cardiff, alongside Frank Lampard and I and he was a great help. But towards the end of that season I think Frank missed being his own man, missed the buzz of management, and took over the hot seat at Cardiff. Roger Cross, who was assistant manager at Tottenham with Gerry Francis, took over from Frank at Upton Park. Roger was in the West Ham youth team with Frank Lampard so we all go back a long way. These are all good men around me and they helped me transform the Hammers fortunes.

I can't stress how important it is to teach youngsters good habits as soon as they arrive at the club. Nowadays we're seeing kids 10 years of age at Upton Park and we've got to start educating them then about diet, preparation and fitness. Fish and chips are out. There could be two players of equal ability on the park but the one who lives right will always have a clear edge. I remember Kenny Dalglish telling me after he'd quit Liverpool so sensationally a few years back that one of the things he found hard to accept was the attitude of some of the senior players. There was a clique who thought the way a professional footballer should live was to finish training and then pile down to a pub near the Liverpool training ground, for an all-day session, leaving only when they couldn't stand up any longer. I think that was a key reason for him leaving the club. He was sickened by the example such behaviour set for the youngsters at Anfield.

Graeme Souness told me a story about his first year playing in Italy for Sampdoria. It was a pre-season friendly up in the mountains on a boiling hot day and Graeme got on the team coach after the game with a small bottle of Peroni, an Italian lager, in his hand. Everything went silent, he said. Every pair of eyes on the coach was upon him. As he got off the coach he was told to report on Monday morning to the club president. 'If you do that again we'll send you back to England', he was told. All for a bottle of Peroni.

CHAPTER 8

The Foreign Legion

I was slated a few years ago for signing up so many foreign mercenaries, players who apparently wanted the big bucks performing in the Premiership could bring, but who had no loyalty towards West Ham Football Club. In some ways the criticism, and it was widespread, was justified, but I will argue long into the night that not all my foreign adventures flopped. Some were big hits, others embarrassing failures, but it's important I put on record just why I had to turn my back on the traditional East End academy at Upton Park and cast my net across Europe in the constant search for top-class players.

There was no doubt going into the 1996–97 Premiership season that the team needed strengthening if we were to avoid another nail-biting fight against relegation. I knew that, the board knew it too, and the fans were all too painfully aware of it. But I had my hands tied. Yes, the team needed reinforcements of the highest quality, but I had to capture them on a shoestring budget. I had no option at that time but to look abroad because even £750,000 for a player in Britain was no guarantee of quality. The transfer market here had gone haywire and a club like West Ham just couldn't afford the astronomical fees. So I looked to Europe. I took a few gambles, and in the main they didn't pay off. But for the first time I was dealing in a market I knew nothing about. I'd always prided myself on being a good judge of a player, but I was having to make snap judgements, sometimes after watching only a half-hour video of a player. It was different for the Chelseas and Arsenals. They were buying internationals of proven calibre; for West Ham it was more your bargain-basement buys. When you look at some of the names I brought to West Ham, it almost makes the mouth water. Unfortunately the performances of some of these players didn't live up to their fancy reputations.

A perfect illustration was Florin Raducioiu, the Romanian international whose Christian name was wonderfully appropriate given that his displays for us were worth about two bob! In the 1990 and 1994 World Cups, Raducioiu was a superstar for Romania, absolutely different class. Here was a player, I thought, who could do brilliantly in the Premiership. I bumped into new Everton boss Walter Smith, then the Rangers manager, on holiday and he told me he had tried to sign Raducioiu six times the previous season but that he didn't want to move to Scotland. And the Romanian manager Anghel Iordanescu told me Raducioiu and Hagi were the two most influential players in his team. Those were pretty sound credentials but, as it turned out, well wide of the mark.

I paid £1.5 million for him, in August 1996, from Spanish club Espanyol and given his pedigree I thought he was well worth the gamble, but I wish now I'd have trusted my initial instincts. I watched Romania play against Bulgaria in Euro '96 and met Raducioiu in a hotel that night for a chat. Rather than discussing his ambitions with West Ham, whether we had realistic European prospects, and what players we would be signing to link up with him, all he wanted to talk about was whether he could bring his dog into the country. He didn't want it put in quarantine, he said, because he and his wife would miss it. This gave me a very nasty feeling. I knew then I should have backed out of the deal, but I was desperate for someone. As I said I didn't have the money to buy a top-quality British striker. We'd all love to go out and buy a Shearer, a Fowler, or a Ferdinand, but I had to be realistic. Raducioiu's concern about his dog really did frighten me and, if you excuse the pun, I should have bowed out there and then. I wish I had.

I worked for a couple of hours with Raducioiu on the first day in training and I must admit he impressed me. He was a quality finisher and I really thought he'd be a success. But the moment we got into anything physical, he didn't want to know. He just couldn't face being tackled in any shape or form. Dicksy was anxious to get stuck in to him to see what he was made of, but Raducioiu made it clear that he wouldn't be challenging for anything. I turned a blind eye at first, thinking things were bound to be different in a match. We went to Torquay for our first pre-season game and I was really looking forward to seeing our big new signing in action. But in the first half he jumped out of the way of every tackle and hardly got a touch of the ball. I asked him at half-time if everything was okay and he said: 'No. They all want to kick me. They are trying to hurt me.' I thought I must have been watching a different game. 'This is England,' I said. 'It's a more physical game. Don't worry, it's no problem.'

Halfway through the second half Raducioiu decided to aim a kick at John Gittins, the Torquay centre half who had a reputation as a bit of a hard nut. But this wasn't a proper kick. It was a little toe-poke, like something a little girl would do, and then he ran away. I saw him do it and knew there would be trouble ahead. Two minutes later, when the ball was up the other end of the pitch, Gittins cracked his elbow into Raducioiu's face and he went down, pole-axed, before starting to scream and cry. Gittins was out of order, but it wasn't that bad a knock. From then on it got worse. At Luton a couple of days later, he pulled the same stunt, complaining that he was getting kicked all the time. Don't ask me to explain how a former world-class player can suddenly become a fairy, but something had obviously happened to Raducioiu and he'd completely lost it. He'd been used to queuing for three hours in Bucharest for a loaf of bread and suddenly he was wearing a £28,000 watch. Perhaps the transition was too much for him.

When the season started I had to play him. I had no one else. The rest of the players didn't take to him. They all thought he was a big tart. I remember Paolo Futre, a new signing from Portugal and not someone you'd imagine easily adapting to the rough and tumble of the Premiership, angrily confronting Raducioiu. He poked him in the chest and said in halting English: 'You are like a big girl. Try being a man.' Players were coming into my office to complain about him.

Surprisingly, though, the West Ham punters seemed to like him. I think they were prepared to give him a chance. They'd seen him perform superbly in the World Cup in USA '94 and probably thought it was only a matter of time before he recaptured that form. Raducioiu came on as sub against Sunderland around Christmas time and scored what everybody classed as a great goal, dummying a defender on the halfway line and running on to score. But I looked at the video of the goal a million times and I can tell you a different story. What everybody saw as this wondrous dummy was in fact Raducioiu jumping out of the way of a challenge. The defender, bamboozled for a minute, missed the ball completely and of course Raducioiu was away. He was quick, I'll give him that, and the thought that at any moment he might be tackled made him quicker still. He took his goal well, I must admit, and the fans were delighted. Against my better judgement I kept him in the team but his performances didn't improve, and I had to relegate him to the bench again. One night in a televised game he came on as substitute against Manchester United at Upton

Park and scored a great goal to earn us a point, and the fans loved him for it. But in my eyes he was a complete non-trier. Raducioiu went on record as saying he wasn't being given a chance by me, and I must admit I took a bit of stick from some of the fans. One or two claimed I couldn't handle big-name players. But the rest of the dressing room had seen through him. They knew what he was like.

The final straw came in a Coca-Cola Cup tie up at Stockport in November. We all met at the Swallow Hotel on the Monday for the coach journey north, but there was no sign of Raducioiu. We all hung around for an hour while we tried to track him down, ringing his hotel, his mobile, the lot. Ilie Dumitrescu, his friend and team-mate in the Romanian national side, made out he didn't have his mate's number, didn't have a clue where he was, but I reckon Ilie knew he wasn't going to turn up. The next day, the day of the match, we tried all day long to contact Raducioiu but without success. It's important to remember that at this time we were really struggling. Results hadn't gone our way, and the Coca-Cola Cup was our big chance to make something of the season, to lift our fans and players. I wouldn't be guilty of exaggeration if I say that things were desperate. It was a massive game for us – we'd drawn 1–1 with County at Upton Park but with no sign of Raducioiu I was forced to play Dumitrescu up front with Iain Dowie in the replay. Things went well early on at Edgeley Park and we took a 1–0 lead. Then Dowie, who hadn't scored a goal for almost 50 games, suddenly thought the time was right to end his famine, but chose to score in the wrong end with a terrible header. Our heads dropped and Stockport beat us 2–1, a result which really piled the pressure on for me.

So you can imagine my mood the next day when a friend rang and told me the previous evening he'd spotted Raducioiu out shopping with his wife in the Harvey Nichols store in London. I knew then I had to get rid of him, but it wasn't easy. Eventually Espanyol, the club we'd signed him from, took him back.

They'd just appointed a new coach, a Romanian, who wanted Raducioiu to return. We got more or less our money back – £1 million. But it didn't take long for Espanyol to bomb him out, and now he's no longer a member of the Romanian side. A career in terminal decline.

It's a toss-up between Raducioiu and Marco Boogers for my 'worst ever foreign signing' tag. Again Boogers arrived at Upton Park as a result of me not having enough money to sign a British striker. I wanted to sign Marcus Stewart from Bristol Rovers but they wanted £1.5 million, and I made one or two other enquiries but I couldn't get anyone. So in the end I went for Boogers for £800,000 from Sparta Rotterdam in Holland. I admit for the first time in my life I signed a player purely on video evidence. Someone sent me a tape of Boogers in action and urged me to watch it. 'He's different class,' I was told. I watched it and was very impressed. Frank Lampard thought the same, so did everyone else at the club. The new season was almost upon us and we didn't have the time to check out Boogers any further so I took the risk and signed him. This turned out to be a big mistake, but the problem was that I didn't know that I was making a mistake at the time. When you sign a foreign player you can never be completely sure of his background. You can't predict if his wife is going to settle, or if the player is going to be homesick. I confess I didn't go into Marco's background too closely, but everyone I spoke to said he was a good player and most foreigners who have come to England have been good professionals.

But right from the word go Boogers' attitude stank. He was among the stragglers at the back whenever we went for a run, he didn't want to work, he was lazy and the players all took an instant dislike to him. I suppose you could say he could play a bit, but certainly he was nowhere near as impressive as the video had made him out to be. Not like it said in the brochure, if you like. Like Raducioiu, he didn't fancy the physical side of the game. He didn't take to the English style of football, hated training, and said his wife couldn't settle. In his first game, against Manchester United, the only kick he had was one at Gary Neville that got him sent off. He was declared 'psychologically unfit for football' – which only meant he'd persuaded a doctor to come up with some excuse why he couldn't return – and disappeared somewhere back home. We eventually found him hiding out in a caravan in Holland and only got him back by reading the riot act. But his attitude was no better when he returned and we got shot of him to Groningen in the Dutch League.

Paolo Futre arrived around the same time as Raducioiu and though he caused one or two problems his ability was never in any doubt. I'd watched Futre star for Portugal for many years and I was delighted when I got him on a free transfer from AC Milan. Derby manager Jim Smith was on the verge of signing him when I nipped in under his nose. Poor old Jim. I don't think he's ever forgiven me for it. One day I got a call from Jerome Anderson, the agent representing Futre in England, and he told me Futre was due to see Jim in Italy the following day. I couldn't believe it when he told me Futre was available on a free. 'He's had a bad injury,' he told me, 'but he's back playing again now.' I asked Jerome if he could arrange an interview with the Portuguese international and we fixed up a meeting at the Post House Hotel at Heathrow Airport at 9am the next morning. At the meeting I was instantly impressed. I could tell he wanted to play football, despite suffering an injury that had at one time threatened his career.

During our chat Futre's mobile phone rang. On the other end of the line was his Italian-based agent wondering where the hell Futre was. He had Jim Smith with him and they'd been searching high and low in Milan for the little Portuguese. Futre managed not to reveal his whereabouts and we went on to complete a deal that suited both parties, with a very important clause: Futre agreed that if he was to suffer any further injuries we could cancel his contract with just a month's notice. His basic wage was good without being astronomical because most of his pay was based on appearances. I had struck a good deal. I drove home feeling very pleased with myself, and grinned further when Sandra told me on the mobile during the journey that Jim Smith had been trying all day to contact me. Seconds later the mobile chirped into life again and it was Jim.

'Harry, where are you?'

'I'm in the car on the way home. Where are you?'

'I'm in Italy,' he said, as if I should have known. 'You haven't by any chance seen Paolo Futre, have you?'

'Who?' I asked, with just the right note of surprise in my voice. Olivier, eat your heart out.

'Paolo Futre,' he repeated. 'I've come to Italy to sign him and he ain't here. Someone said he was talking to you.'

Now I love Smithy, he's a good mate, so I couldn't lie to him any further. 'As it happens, Smithy, I've just met him at Heathrow Airport.'

'What?' he roared. 'You can't have. He's supposed to be here. We're all here to sign him.'

'Too late, Jim. He's just signed for West Ham.'

The air went blue. He went berserk. You can just imagine that face getting redder and redder. 'Don't worry Jim,' I said. 'I'll send you a nice bottle of red wine,' and put the phone down with Smithy still effing and blinding.

Futre was a winner. He'd suffered a bad knee injury and his best days were probably behind him but he wanted to play, wanted to train, and wanted to get fit. He'd captained Portugal, revelled in responsibility, and cared deeply about doing well for whatever club he played for. But all the time he carried his knee. You could tell it was always on his mind. For 10 minutes he would do things you'd never seen in your life. He'd beat two or three players with an outrageous turn or feint, but he couldn't sustain it. You wouldn't see him for the next 20 minutes, he'd be stood still. I admired his attitude, although the story I'm about to recount should have made me question it.

It was the first League game of the 1996–97 season and we were up at Arsenal. I handed the team-sheet into the referee's room but when I got back to the dressing room Eddie Gillam, our trainer, told me we had a problem with Paolo and the shirts.

'What kind of problem,' I asked, innocently. 'Doesn't it fit him?'

But it was a lot more serious than that. We'd allocated number 16 to Futre, but he thought such a shirt was an insult.

'Futre,' he said, pointing to his chest. 'Futre number 10.'

I explained to him that he had to wear number 16, that it wasn't like the old days when players could wear different numbers every week, that it was FA rules that players were allocated a squad number at the beginning of the season and were stuck with it. But I may as well have recited a nursery rhyme. 'Futre,' he shouted, jabbing his chest again. 'Futre. Eusebio number 10. Futre number 10.'

'Yeah I understand all that,' I said, 'but there's nothing we can do. Moncur is number 10. You are number 16. We can't change it now.'

'No f****** way 16,' Futre said, his voice rising further. 'F****** number 10.'

By this stage there were only about 45 minutes to the kick-off, the sun was shining, and thousands of fans at Highbury were looking forward excitedly to the new season.

'Look,' I said. 'Just wear the number 16 shirt and go out and play. We'll talk about it later.'

But he wouldn't have it. By this time the commotion had attracted the attention of the other players and they all looked to see what was going on, while pretending to prepare for the match.

'Okay then,' I said. 'What are you going to do?'

'F*** off,' he said. 'No play.'

I'd heard enough. I used Futre's colourful expressions to tell him where to go and next minute he was off, in a cab and home. But that wasn't the end of the problem. I then had to go back to the referee and tell him we'd made a mistake with the team-sheet.

'Ref,' I said. 'I've just noticed a bit of a problem with the team-sheet. Frank Lampard's put Paolo Futre down at number 16 but the geezer's not fit. He's not even here. He's in Portugal having treatment.' The ref said it was okay with him to make the change so long as Arsenal agreed, which they did.

The following Monday I hauled Futre into my office. We'd been well turned over at Highbury – John Hartson scored one of Arsenal's two goals – and I honestly didn't care if I never saw Futre again. He had his lawyer and his agent with him and started going into one again about wearing number 10. I'd had more than enough and I think Futre realized pretty quickly from my reactions that he wasn't going to get his own way.

I told him that in England kids buy football shirts with the name and number of their favourite player. John Moncur was number 10. It couldn't be changed. Too many shirts had been sold.

'How many?' Futre asked. 'How much money?'

'A hundred thousand pounds' worth,' I said. In truth we'd probably sold about six.

'I pay,' he said. 'I pay. I give £100,000 and you take the shirts back. Give them the money back.'

I couldn't believe it. He wanted to fork out 100 grand just to wear the number 10. I suppose in a way you had to admire his principles. In the end I said I'd talk to Moncur to find out his feelings. Then Futre offered an irresistible sweetener. He owned a villa, reportedly one of the most luxurious in Portugal, on a clifftop on the coast, with a plush golf course on hand, and offered Moncur a fortnight there free if he handed over his No 10 shirt. To be honest I don't think Moncur gave a monkey's what number he wore, but he took the free holiday, and all we had to do was square the change of number with the FA. Everybody was happy, and the crisis was averted.

Futre was a massive talent but he struggled in the

Premiership. He turned one or two games for us where he was different class but the knee injury did for him. I remember we were at Sunderland in a howling wind with him, Dumitrescu and Raducioiu up front. Sunderland were swarming in on our goal and the three of them were standing there on the halfway line looking on. I knew then it wasn't going to work long term.

Despite the few problems with Futre, all in all Portugal was a bit of a happy hunting ground. We got Hugo Porfirio on loan from Sporting Lisbon for a year and he was a big hit with our fans. We offered him a deal to stay but he got offered massive money from Spain and we couldn't hang onto him. And before that we had Dani, who was a terrific young player and set us alight for a short time. He scored at Tottenham in February that season, a game which probably kept us up, but his club Sporting Lisbon wanted £5 million for him and there was no way we could afford that. Dani was a big hit with the girls. A real glamour boy with film-star looks. I remember him coming out for training in the freezing cold, and while all the other players had woollen hats pulled down over their ears, Dani would wear a designer bobble hat with suede in the middle.

His playboy image was best highlighted when I took the players to Tenerife for a mid-season break to get away from the pressures of the relegation battle. It was a blank week because England were playing and I thought a spell in the sunshine would recharge our batteries. I warned the lads we were there to keep fit, swim, play tennis, and train hard, and we weren't there to get drunk or hang around in night clubs. I made it clear that if I found anyone taking liberties I would hammer them. 'Go out tonight,' I said, 'and enjoy yourselves, but 9.30 in the morning I want you all down for training.' The next morning down in the lobby all the lads were there except for Dani, who was supposed to be sharing a room with a young Irish lad called Graeme Philson.

'Where's Dani?' I asked Graeme.

'I dunno,' he said. 'Haven't seen him.'

So we went training minus our little Portuguese film star. Come 1.30pm and there was still no sign of him. I'd worked the lads hard in the morning and by now we were all relaxing by the pool in the sunshine. Suddenly, there's this tanned figure walking towards us, hair immaculate, sun-glasses on, every inch the film star. It was Dani.

'Where've you been?' I demanded.

But he couldn't, or rather wouldn't, give me an explanation. All the lads knew he'd picked up a bird, maybe even two or three, the night before, but there was no way he was going to tell me that.

'I'm fining you £1,000,' I said. 'I warned you there'd be trouble if you didn't show up for training. That's £1,000 I'm fining you.' He looked at me and smiled. 'Aah, thank you coach,' he said. 'Thank you. Thank you,' and walked off. I turned to Frank Lampard and said: 'He must have had a good night last night if it was worth a grand.' He'd walked away happy as a sand boy, as though I'd done him a favour. It just shows that nowadays a grand is nothing to a top footballer. But he was a good player and a nice lad, was Dani.

When he first came over to West Ham we put him up in the Swallow Hotel in Waltham Abbey. A couple of days later he came up to me and said: 'Coach. Hotel no good. I have found another.'

'The Swallow Hotel is a good hotel,' I said. 'Everybody stays there. When Manchester United are in London, that's where they stay.' But this didn't wash with Dani. He'd found somewhere else.

'Okay, which one is it?' I asked.

'The Dorchester,' he said. 'My friend say is very good."

'The Dorchester,' I said, amazed. 'Do me a favour. Who told you about that one?'

'My friend, coach. I want the Dorchester. I want to see the sights.'

'Yeah, I bet you do,' I said. 'You're not having the Dorchester.'

Next day he said he wanted to stay in The Tower Hotel, but even when we got him a mini-suite he wasn't happy. It wasn't big enough for him. God knows what he was doing in there. In the end we rented him a flat in London's Docklands, just a couple of doors away from Marc Rieper. Marc was a model professional and I asked him to keep an eye on Dani, to make sure he got out of bed in the morning, and it all worked out well.

While I admit that Raducioiu and Boogers were disastrous signings, there were successes in my foreign policy too, namely Slaven Bilic and Marc Rieper. I spotted Bilic playing for Karlsruhe in Germany but after my previous tortures with foreign players there was no way I was going to sign him without first having him over on a trial basis to get to know what he was like. So Slaven came over and after two days I knew all I needed to know. This bloke could play. He had something about him, a certain quality that we badly needed. He played a couple of reserve games and did more than enough to convince me to sign him for £1.5 million. We were later to get £4.5 million for him in a deal that completely changed the fortunes of West Ham for the better.

Rieper came over on loan from Brondby and did tremendously well for us. We had him for two years and in all that time he didn't give me a moment's trouble. He was a perfect pro. We made a profit on him when we sold him to Celtic and it was great to see him performing so well for Denmark in the 1998 World Cup.

I suppose there was a feeling among West Ham supporters when we signed all these foreigners that they were all on mega-wages, but this was not true. They were getting paid a bit more than West Ham was used to, but compared to the way wages today have spiralled beyond control in the Premiership their pay was nothing special. The manner of transfer dealings with continental clubs suited West Ham. When you buy a player in England you have to pay 50 per cent of the fee up front and the remainder over a year. To buy a striker for £3million means having to come up with £1.5 million straight away. But for the same deal abroad you could put maybe £300,000 down, or even pay the first instalment after three months. There's so much more flexibility.

But there was a problem, I'd have to admit, with team spirit. I ended up with just too many foreign players, and all the talk in the press about the Foreign Legion this and the League of Nations that began to affect supporters and players. Raducioiu wasn't popular, as I've said, and nor was Boogers, but overall the dressing room was too quiet. Dicksy was the captain but off the pitch he's a quiet lad. He's not a voice in the dressing room, or even on the pitch for that matter, but as a captain he led by example, by the way he played. Bilic was a presence, so too Dowie, but we needed more of them. I think I realized about then that I'd overdone the continental flavour.

Looking back at this madcap period of foreign risk-taking I have mixed feelings. As I've outlined, some of these signings were unmitigated disasters but the bright spots were plenty. It's not hard to sign a Bergkamp for £7 million or a Zola for £5 million because you are buying proven quality. It's when you are dealing at the other end of the market that you're in trouble. You're always gambling. I was buying second-hand players with no MOTs. It was an experience, something I can almost laugh at now, and you've got to remember the successes cancelled out the failures. You can say the £4.5 million we got for Bilic more than compensated for those signings that didn't come off. So it wasn't as if it was all a financial disaster for the club. At the time I had no money, my hands were tied, and I had to take some gambles. But as you know by now, I've been doing that all my life.

The media said buying John Hartson and Paul Kitson for a combined fee of £5.5 million was a desperate gamble, the last throw of the dice for a doomed manager, but I just wonder what West Ham fans would have made of the signing I had planned before I plunged for them. I was told of a South American player who was a goalscoring sensation, and who was available for £3 million. He agreed to come over to West Ham for a trial period but broke his toe just before he was due to arrive and I went for the two Brits instead. His name? Marcelo Salas, the Chilean hit-man who scored that wonder goal against England at Wembley and who was one of the stars of France '98. Estimated value now? About £20 million. What would they have said about my foreign policy then?

CHAPTER 9

Buying British

It was midway through the 1996–97 season, and the phone trilled at West Ham's training ground, as it does every minute of the day. It was Tottenham manager Gerry Francis. 'I'll give you £2.5 million for Slaven Bilic,' he said.

What the hell is going on, I thought. Our place in the Premiership is hardly safe, a relegation battle later in the season is a real prospect, and now someone expects me to sell my best player. 'No way, Gerry,' I told him. 'He's a terrific player and we need him if we're going to stay up. No way will I sell him.'

'But haven't you got to sell him?' he asked. Where had he heard that, I wondered.

'Well you know how it is Harry,' Francis went on. 'An agent has told us Bilic has a clause in his contract that says if a club offers £2.5 million for him you've got to sell him.'

'You've got that wrong, Gerry,' I said, and the conversation moved on.

A couple of days later, Bilic came into my office to see me. He moaned about how the club was struggling, how we had no money to buy new players, how he wanted to join a bigger club, and finished by saying he'd heard Tottenham had made an offer for him. I told him they had, for £2.5 million.

'Well in that case you must sell me,' he said. 'Look at my contract. It says so.'

'I've read your contract,' I said, 'and it says that if we get an offer of £2.5 million or more and we want to sell you and you want to go, then the deal goes through.'

'That is settled then,' he said.

'But *we* don't want to sell you.'

It took a few seconds for this news to sink in with Bilic. Then he reacted angrily. 'No, no, no. This is wrong. This is very wrong. You have tricked me.'

Bilic is a fully qualified lawyer and must have thought his contract was watertight. But I went to the University of the Street in Stepney and I had done him up like a kipper.

Bilic had the hump big time, but I told him it was his own fault. 'You're a lawyer,' I said. 'You should have read your contract properly.' But those words were not exactly guaranteed to pacify him. He kept moaning how much he could be earning at a bigger club so in the end we agreed to give him a new contract, making him the best-paid player at West Ham by miles. He had a clause inserted that if a club offered anything over £4.5 million for him, we would have to sell, whether we liked it or not. I was happy with that. I thought £4.5 million was good money for a defender, particularly one 28 years old.

By this time our season was beginning to fall apart around our ears and we were in desperate trouble. One morning the phone rang. It was Joe Royle, the Everton manager.

'Hello Harry. You're not going to want to hear this. We want to buy Slaven Bilic.'

I knew what was coming as Joe went on: 'We know his

contract says you've got to release him if we offer £4.5 million. I don't want to screw you, Harry. We get on great, but business is business and we do want him.' There was nothing I could do. I said to Bilic the next day, perhaps hoping to appeal to his better instincts, that there were only 12 games to go to the end of the season and that we were in dire trouble, so was he going to leave us in the lurch?

'I am a professional,' he said. 'I have to do what I have to do. If they make me an offer that I am happy with, then I will sign.' I suppose I couldn't argue, but as Bilic walked out of the door, so too did my already slender hopes of avoiding the drop. But something about my demeanour must have pricked Bilic's conscience. He went to Goodison to meet Joe Royle and the two camps agreed terms. But for some reason Everton, who looked 100 per cent safe at that stage, agreed to allow him to stay at West Ham until the end of the season. The deal was signed, sealed and delivered, but Bilic stayed until the end of the campaign. In all honesty he had money owing to him from West Ham, a signing-on fee from when he originally joined us, so maybe that had something to do with his decision to hang around. Maybe he believed he had a better chance of being paid what was owed if he offered to help our relegation battle, but all credit to Bilic, he came back and gave us 100 per cent throughout the closing weeks of the season. He helped to keep us up, and I really couldn't have asked for anything more from him.

The ironic thing was that Everton got sucked into the relegation battle as well. With two or three games to go they looked like they might go down, and poor old Bilic was anxious to hear the Everton result as soon as our match had finished. As it turned out the Bilic deal was the best thing that could have happened to us. He was able to stay and help out in our relegation dogfight and, more importantly, the money we got for him enabled us to go out and sign John Hartson and

Paul Kitson, the two men most responsible for keeping West Ham in the top flight at the end of the 1996–97 season.

Morale in the camp was at a very low ebb. The foreign adventure had not paid off and once we had off-loaded most of them we were left with a squad too thin to keep us in the Premiership. I told the chairman that there was no way the club would avoid relegation, not with the players we had at our disposal. To be fair to him he took that warning to heart and once the Bilic deal was done he gave me the go-ahead to sign two strikers. That had been our major problem that season. We just never looked like scoring.

I rang Arsenal and asked if they were willing to sell Hartson, who was only on the fringe of the first team. To my surprise they said they were so I wasted no time in fixing up a meeting with John. Within 10 minutes he'd signed, no messing about whatsoever. 'Yeah, I'd love to play for you, Harry. Love to play for the Hammers', he said. And the deal was done. I'd been impressed with Hartson each time I'd seen him. He was young, barely 21, and big and strong. He gave us a presence that we were lacking. Initially I wanted Pierre Van Hooijdonk, the Dutch international who had proved a tremendous signing for Nottingham Forest, until all that contractual trouble at the start of the 1998–99 season. I went up to Celtic three times to watch him, but the way he played put me off a little. He always wanted to play too deep, to score his goals from 25 yards. I needed someone who was going to play more in the box for me. To get up there, to hold the ball up, to be a threat whenever the ball was in the opposition penalty area. Van Hooijdonk wasn't like that; Hartson most certainly was and in the end I went for him, for £3 million, and what a bargain buy he has proved.

Yet when I signed him all hell let loose at what was seen as an inflated price tag. You wouldn't believe the stick John took, which was ridiculously unfair. All he'd done was sign for another club; he had no say in the transfer fee. Outspoken radio DJ Danny Baker was one of the fiercest critics. He called John a donkey and urged the fans to boo him in his first match against Derby. Everybody slaughtered him. Yet I knew it wasn't the reckless gamble everybody was saying. I knew he'd do a good job for the club. It was the same with Paul Kitson, who at the time couldn't get a game in the Newcastle first team. Quite a few people warned me off Kitson. He's a moody, miserable git, they said. Don't touch him with a barge pole. But I liked him when we met and I thought he'd work well with Hartson. Once we clinched the signing of those two, for a total of about £5.5 million, I thought we'd stay up, even though we looked in an impossible situation. Yes it was a lot of dough for a club like West Ham. The chairman really pushed the boat out, but remember we had £4.5 million due from the Bilic deal, and desperate situations called for desperate remedies. He knew as well as I did that if we didn't spend we'd die.

We were at Derby on 15 February for Hartson's first game. In all the stick that had been levelled at him when he signed, much was made of his suspect disciplinary record and I must admit he was a bit of a hot-head. Early on at Derby he went up for a header with Rams defender Igor Stimac. It was a fair challenge, no doubt about it, but Stimac started staggering about all over the field as though his legs had turned to jelly. After about a 40-yard wobble he fell over in a heap. The crowd went mad but the ref just told him to get up. He knew there was nothing wrong with him. But Stimac wouldn't get to his feet, continuing to play the wounded soldier. By now the ref had to stop the game and still the Derby crowd were going berserk. Stimac finally got up, walked 15 yards, and promptly fell over again. So for some reason the ref then booked Hartson and that got him suspended for two games because of an earlier yellow card he'd picked up while with

Arsenal. You can imagine the critics. Baker gave it the large one: 'I told you about Hartson. One game for West Ham and he's already suspended. What a waste of money.' The pressure on the lad was getting ridiculous and I was taking flak as well.

In our next game we were at home to Tottenham in a live Sky match on a Monday night. It must have been the game of the season, a 4–3 win for us in pouring rain, with the lead swinging one way then the other. Hartson and Kitson were fantastic. They both got a goal, with Julian Dicks – back with the club after an unhappy spell at Liverpool – weighing in with a couple, one from the penalty spot. And that was the turning point. No one could stop us. Wherever we played we scored. Suddenly we were coming from behind in games because the players believed we could score. Previously if we'd gone 1–0 down we may as well have gone home. We went 1–0 down at Coventry in a crucial relegation battle, Rieper putting through his own goal in the first 10 minutes, but came back to win 3–1 with Hartson grabbing a couple, and that was the way our season went in the closing weeks. The turnaround was unbelievable. Even those warnings about the moody Kitson were unfounded. He can be a bit dour, but all the players like him and to me he's one of the lads.

In April that year I brought Steve Lomas in from Manchester City and he did a great job for us. Hartson and Kitson take most of the credit for keeping us up but Lomas was equally influential in that great escape. He got after people, tackled, worked, put his foot in, and suddenly it was a different team. He gave us something we hadn't had – a genuine ball-winner in midfield who got around the pitch, and he added much-needed bite.

I should also mention here the service to West Ham of Iain Dowie, who I rate one of my best-ever signings. Few people have taken more criticism during my time as West Ham manager than Iain. I know he didn't have the best of records in front of goal, but I would stand up for him anywhere, any time. I bought Dowie from Crystal Palace for £250,000 the season before the great Upton Park foreign influx. He'd had a spell at the club before and by all accounts was not a great success but I was keen to bring him back. Everybody at the club said I was a fool because the fans hated him. The chairman even said he and I would be a laughing stock if he returned. But I said I didn't care. I liked what I saw. Dowie was an honest pro who I could see doing a good job for us. And that year he was fantastic. He scored several important goals for us and was one of the main reasons we stayed up. In fact his form that season made most of the fans eat their words and he was runner-up for the Hammer Of The Year award. He led the line well, he was a presence in the dressing room, he put himself about for us, and opposing defenders hated playing against him. He was a great signing for us, and I'm happy to put that on record.

The performances of these players saved our season, but even when the results turned our way the pressure was still on. I don't look back on those months with any pleasure. Even when we looked like we were going to be safe, me and Frank Lampard couldn't relax. We needed Middlesbrough not to win at Blackburn on the Thursday night before the final weekend of the season to guarantee our safety. That night we took our wives out for dinner, to try to take our minds off it, but we just couldn't switch off. We spent the whole evening listening to the commentary from Ewood Park on Clubcall, each of us looking intently at the face of whoever held the receiver for a clue to what was happening. They say don't take it home with you but I couldn't do anything else. That's the way I am. Thankfully, a traumatic season ended with us guaranteeing our Premiership future. But it's a season I'll never forget – so few highs, and so many lows. And I still vividly remember staring into the abyss the night we lost to

Wrexham in the FA Cup in January that year. I'd been on the happier side of giant-killing acts when I was at Bournemouth but this was the first time in management I'd been on the receiving end. There aren't many worse feelings. Yet though the crowd demonstrated against the board – this was at the time of the proposed take-over of the club by millionaire racehorse owner Michael Tabor – I escaped the worst of the criticism. It was a combination of the Cup defeat, the stress it was causing both myself and my wife, and the boardroom struggle with Tabor that eventually forced me to tender my resignation – a move I will elaborate on shortly.

I'm a keen gambler, but compared to a high-roller like Michael Tabor, I bet in pennies. Tabor is the man who almost took over control of West Ham during those dark days of the winter of 1996–97. He is also one of the biggest names in racing, and owner of a string of the very highest-class racehorses. I'd known Tabor, a West Ham supporter, for a few years when he told me he'd be interested in taking control at Upton Park. Things were tight, the team was struggling, but the board seemed to give the impression that they'd done enough, that they'd given all the backing they could, and that no more money would be made available to strengthen the squad. I knew that if we were going to push on, to improve our status after years of yo-yoing between the top two divisions, it was essential that we found more financial clout.

I mentioned Tabor's interest to Peter Storrie, and he and the chairman seemed quite keen. Tabor invited the three of us to his box at the three-day Cheltenham Festival, along with a string of top racing figures like Vincent O'Brien, Christy Roche, John Magnier, and perhaps the most fearless punter in Britain, JP McManus. Neither the chairman nor Peter are gambling men and they knew nothing of these colourful turf characters who to all intents and purposes inhabit a different world.

Tabor is a rich man, seriously rich, and he employs a chap, a Mr Fix-it if you like, who goes everywhere with him, organizing hotels, food, tables, champagne, the lot. This chap, an Irishman, welcomed the three-man West Ham party to Tabor's private box at Cheltenham and sat us down, with the chairman opposite Tabor. Then he brought us drinks, served our food, and generally looked after us and made us feel very welcome. After about 15 minutes Tabor had to leave the table to take a phone call, and the chairman whispered to me: 'Who is that man?' pointing towards the disappearing figure of Tabor.

'That's Michael Tabor.'

'How can that be Michael Tabor,' he said, '*That's* Michael Tabor,' pointing at the little Irish feller. I had to laugh. One of the wealthiest men around and our chairman thought he was serving 30 people their grub, dolloping spuds on our plate. Not a great start.

Anyway, we went back for dinner at the hotel the chairman was staying at in Warwickshire. Discussions continued and everything seemed to be going fine. 'This could be a goer,' I thought. But somewhere along the line it all went wrong.

Tabor had a solicitor in London who got involved and I don't think his forthright approach was appreciated. Tabor made an offer for so many shares which the chairman did not find acceptable, and all of a sudden relations between the two groups were not the most cordial. I think the offer was £30 million, of which about £22 million was on a loan basis. Tabor kept setting deadlines, the chairman didn't respond to them, and then Tabor would go public on how he was being ignored. Tabor wanted shareholders to oppose the chairman's re-election at the club's AGM in December 1996 and vote in his solicitor, Henry Montlake. But his motion was defeated. All this time unrest among the fans was growing.

The bickering between the two camps got worse and, in all honesty, I don't think it could have helped the team. Although as professionals they should have been able to put off-the-pitch problems behind them. A press report from the time gives a good example of the ill-feeling between Tabor's camp and the chairman.

The Sun, 31 January 1997: 'Michael Tabor has called on people power to sweep him into West Ham. The millionaire ex-bookie wants shareholders of the troubled club to take control from the board. He fears there is little chance of chairman Terence Brown and his directors doing business with him. And he is worried for the club's future, warning it will sink into the First Division unless his £30 million cash injection is accepted. A statement issued by his solicitors last night read: "It is about time small and large shareholders took back control of their company from this Board before the increasing debt brings about the total demise of this club. If enough shareholders indicate support, consideration will be given to calling an Extraordinary General Meeting with a view to furthering the shareholders and fans and getting the company back under proper control."'

In the same article, Peter hit back at Tabor, saying his bid would put the club in debt. The paper reported Peter as saying: 'No one gives you £30 million with no strings attached but that's what the fans are thinking. The fans hear Michael Tabor is prepared to put that amount into the club, but between £22 million and £23 million of it is interest-bearing loans. And he thinks the rest of the money would entitle him to one-third of the shares in the club.'

When Tabor had first met the chairman, West Ham had been playing well, but now, a year on, we were struggling badly. It was around this time – January 1997 – that we lost to Second Division Wrexham at Upton Park in the third round of the FA Cup and morale was at its lowest ebb. The fans turned on the board and wanted them out. I was feeling so low, with little hope of getting us out of trouble, that I offered to quit. A joke doing the rounds about then summed up the air of pessimism at the club perfectly. It was about me walking into a building society and suddenly collapsing. Brought round by a cashier I mumble: 'What happened. Am I in the Nationwide?' 'No,' comes a reassuring voice. 'But you will be next season.'

We were 18th in the Premiership, with one win in 15 games, and had just been beaten by Wrexham at the first hurdle in the FA Cup. Things couldn't get much worse. Fans were demonstrating, making it known they wanted the board out and Tabor in.

'Look,' I said to the chairman. 'It hasn't worked out. You probably feel I'm responsible for the Tabor situation, which is hardly helping things. I know you've got the best interests of the club at heart so maybe it's best if I call it a day.'

To be honest we'd had a couple of meetings before then which had got out of hand, a little bit personal. Deep down I think he thought I wanted him out and Tabor in, and he said one thing to me which I found incredible. Don't get me wrong, the chairman of West Ham has been brilliant to me, but he was out of order on this occasion.

'I wonder if you're trying to get us relegated so your friend Michael Tabor can buy the club cheap,' he said.

Can you imagine the effect of those words on me? There I was coming home every Saturday night making Sandra ill, myself ill, making the lives of all those around me a misery because I took things so seriously, and there's the chairman saying that to me. If I was to recount what I said in reply this page would be covered in asterisks, so let's just say that I left the chairman in no doubt about how I felt about his comment.

To be fair to the chairman though, when I offered to resign

he wouldn't hear of it. He said he thought I was the best man for the job and that he was confident I'd turn things round. From then he was as good as gold to me. I have a good job at West Ham. The chairman doesn't interfere, doesn't poke his nose in where it's not wanted. And that's not the case with all chairmen in the Premiership. He backs everything I want to do and all in all I've been very lucky.

It's possible that even though Michael Tabor's interest in the club ultimately came to nothing, it indirectly saved us from relegation. That's a sweeping statement to make but bear with me. At the time I offered to quit, we were plummeting towards relegation. We couldn't have stayed up. I just didn't have the players to win games. I didn't have a forward who could score goals. I had Mike Newell on loan who had been a great player at Everton and Blackburn but he wasn't the player he was four years earlier. Mike was up front with Steve Jones, who's now at Charlton. We made some money on Jonesey. We bought him from Billericay for £18,000, sold him to Bournemouth for £200,000, bought him back again for the same price, then sold him to Charlton for £400,000. He was a good player, like Newell, but we weren't going to stay up with that pairing. Looking back I think the fans clamouring for Tabor's money, and my offer to resign, perhaps forced the chairman's hand. He knew we'd go down unless drastic action was taken, and all of a sudden he found the money to buy John Hartson and Paul Kitson, plus Steve Lomas, three signings which kept us up and gave us the springboard to do so well the following season.

I still see Michael Tabor from time to time, normally when he invites me to a day's racing. I've always found him a perfect gentleman. He'll ask how the team's doing but he will never quiz me about the goings-on behind the scenes. To be honest he's more interested in the racing. I last bumped into him in Monte Carlo in May, 1998. Not in a casino, before you ask. It was in a restaurant after I'd watched a Monaco game. It was the night of the Eurovision Song Contest and I'd already backed Israel at 12-1 after being given a hot tip while up in Liverpool the week before. I told Michael about the tip but though he bets on just about everything, he wasn't tempted. You should have seen his face when Israel got up on the line. Given the identity of the Israeli representative – no, it wasn't Eyal Berkovic singing *Money Money Money*; it was a girl who used to be a boy – I'd have thought Israel was the perfect each-way bet!

CHAPTER 10

Gambling in the Blood

To this day there are thousands of football supporters who still talk about the betting background to the Manchester United v West Ham match at the end of the 1996–97 season. Think of all the big moments in football history: Geoff Hurst's did-it-cross-the-line goal in the 1966 World Cup Final, Maradona's Hand Of God goal against England in the '86 World Cup, the famous Pele shot from the halfway line. To that little list add the infamous tale of the West Ham throw-in. If I'd only known the stink our unsuccessful opening gambit in that match was to cause, I'd have gladly let United kick-off. It was a match with nothing at stake. United had already been crowned Premiership champions and our survival in the top flight was already guaranteed. Straight from the kick-off Paul Kitson tried to find Iain Dowie with a long ball to the left wing but succeeded only in finding touch. Looking at the replays of his attempted pass, I'd have to admit it wasn't Kitson's most elegant ball but at the time nobody thought anything of it. The game was barely seconds old, players take time to find their touch. In the days after the game, however, all hell let loose. The reason? Spread betting.

Spread betting is perhaps the fastest-growing form of punting in Britain and at the time a popular spread market was betting on the time of the first throw-in in Premiership matches. For example, the spread bookies would estimate the time of the first throw-in at, say, 65-80 seconds, and punters had to bet whether it would be sooner or later than that. If they 'sold' (that is, bet on an earlier throw-in) at 65 seconds and the first throw was timed at five seconds, then they would win 60 times their stake. So we're talking potentially big money here.

The match, or at least our poxy kick-off, would have long been forgotten had it not been for a story in the *Racing Post* the following week. Spread firm Sporting Index apparently reported a large number of sellers at 65 seconds, forcing the line down to 50-65. The inference was clear: someone had cleaned up at the bookies' expense, and the finger of suspicion was pointing at West Ham. The press went mad. The story was picked up by all the national papers and Kitson's misplaced pass, looking worse and worse the more you saw it, was replayed endlessly on TV. I suppose I'd have to admit the circumstantial evidence was pretty strong, but believe me that's all it was – circumstantial.

It's clear the market was open to manipulation – I believe the spread firms were asked to scrap it during the investigation by Sir John Smith into football betting in 1997 – but if you look at the characters involved in this supposed coup you'd realize it was all a cock-and-bull story. There are no punters at West Ham apart from John Hartson, and he wasn't even playing that day; and Paul Kitson knows as much about betting as I do about nuclear science. I didn't even have a spread betting account. And who won this small fortune? Sporting Index claimed they saw a large number of sellers but they later said little damage had been done.

Our kick-off that day was one we and indeed most clubs in the Premiership follow regularly. It just didn't come off, that's all. The betting riddle made a good story, sure, but there was nothing in it. And even if there was, do you think I'd ever admit it? They'd lock me up.

To be honest there's a lot of rubbish talked about football and betting. In my opinion, Sir John Smith's report, which barred all players and managers from betting on football, was a joke. He said he had hard evidence of players betting against their teams, but why didn't he name names? It's like me telling police I know someone who's committed a burglary but I can't let them know who it is because it's confidential. What a load of cobblers. I know plenty of people in this game and I know who the big punters are. Let me tell you there aren't many, and there are none doing their brains every weekend. The days of Stan Bowles, the former England international and legendary gambler, are over.

The report, in theory, stopped me having my weekend bet on the football coupons. Why? What harm was I doing? And does Sir John really believe that his report has stopped players from gambling on the game? You only have to look at Paul Merson's comments when he left Middlesbrough to sign for Aston Villa to see that betting, albeit to small stakes, is a way of life in football.

If they want to bet, they will, just as jockeys will find a way to bet on horseracing even though they are banned from doing so. To bet against your own team is completely and utterly wrong and anyone caught doing it should be punished, but for the life of me I can't see any problem in backing yourself or a team-mate to score the first goal in a game. I know Michael Owen's dad backs him to score the first goal in every Liverpool game and Michael, a keen punter himself, has the same bet, or at least did until the Smith Report. Where's the harm in that? It's not as if the other 21 players are purposely going to miss chances themselves just so they'll get a bet up. There was a big hullabaloo not that long ago about John Scales backing himself at 50–1 to score the first goal in a game. But the only reason there was a big stink was that John actually did open the scoring. What about all the other 50 weeks when his bet lost?

I suppose the FA had two chief concerns. First, to stop any other players getting into the kind of trouble Paul Merson and later Keith Gillespie found themselves in through gambling. Second, to rule out any chance of matches being fixed. But banning players from betting on football won't prevent another Merson incident. There are plenty of other things to bet on. And the spectre of fixed matches, while still a worry, no longer casts the shadow it used to back in the 1960s. Like most football fans I watched *The Fix*, the play on TV in 1997 charting the sad story of Tony Kaye and the other players caught in that dreadful match-fixing scandal. But remember that wages for players in those days were in most cases ordinary. Nowadays the rewards are too great for players to be lured into anything underhand.

Betting plays a large part in my life, even though Sandra frowns upon it. I think gambling was the downfall of her grandad, and her mum who felt the effects of that addiction wanted to make sure her daughter was kept well away. I remember when Sandra and I were first going out. I picked her up from work in a hairdresser's one Friday and took her home. I left there and shot off to the dog-track. Anyway, when I called round to Sandra's the next evening, her dad, a foreman in the docks, great big geezer, began to quiz me.

'Where did you go last night when you left here?' he barked.

'Hang about', I said. 'What business is it of yours?'

'You went to the dogs,' he said, glaring at me. It turned out he and Sandra's brother had followed me in their van when I left, all the way to the dog-track. Can you believe it? 'You're supposed to be saving up to buy a house,' he said. 'I don't want you messing around with my daughter if you're going to waste your money gambling.'

I have a father whose every waking moment revolves around football even though he's now in his seventies, so it's perhaps no surprise that the sport has been my living for more than 30 years. But it was equally inevitable that gambling would be in my blood given the influence of my nan Maggie Brown, my mum's mother. What a character she was. I used to rush home from school every day to my nan's for dinner and the first thing she did was put the *Mid-day Star*, or the *Mid-day Standard* as it was in those days, in front of me and ask me to pick out three horses. I couldn't even read or write but she'd put a pen in my hand and ask me to mark three selections. Then she'd pick up the paper, rub it on my head – 'Ginger for luck,' she'd say – and wait for Cyril the paper-boy, also known as Cyril the bookie, to come round. My nan was a bookie's runner. She'd go round the whole street collecting bets and then pass them on to Cyril. The people in the neighbourhood would write their bets on little bits of paper and put their names on the bottom. That was how they'd bet. Three tuppeny doubles and a tuppeny treble. My nan would have them all on the mantelpiece, and when Cyril came round with the paper, she'd have the bets wrapped up individually and drop them in Cyril's satchel. His paper round was just a front for his bookmaking because being a bookie was illegal in those days, as was being a bookie's runner.

I'd come home from school for dinner and quite often my nan would be getting carted away in a police car. 'Your dinner's in the oven,' she'd shout to me. 'These bastards won't keep me for long. I'll be home in an hour, boy.' The police would have her down the station for a couple of hours, warn her off, and then she'd come back and do exactly the same as before. They never put her off. She loved it. But somehow her gambling instincts were never picked up by my mum. She's not a gambler, although she will have a bet on the Derby and

Grand National. And my dad's not a punter at all. He just lives for football.

My dad was a docker and my mum worked in the Co-op. I was an only child, which I suppose was unusual for those days, and one of my most vivid memories from my childhood was following my dad, Harry Snr, all over the place to watch him play football. My old man was a terrific footballer. I know lots of people say they could have made it as a professional but I'm not kidding you when I say he had terrific ability. He only played in the local Business Houses league but he was far, far better than that. I remember one year in the late Seventies we spent a weekend in a caravan in the Isle Of Sheppey. Frank (Lampard) had just been picked for England, but in a little kickabout we had he couldn't get the ball off my dad, who must have been about 55 at the time. He would nutmeg him, drag the ball, and Frank, one way then the other. He ran Frank silly. Even now, at 74, he can do anything with a ball.

My dad had a rough life as a kid. His mum and dad died when he was about 15, and he was in the army a year later. He was a POW during the Second World War, and I think by the time it ended he'd perhaps missed his chance to make a name for himself in football. All the top amateur teams in London kept asking him to play for them but he was happy playing with his mates. Even today he's football mad, the ultimate football loon. Around his neighbourhood if there's a game on my old man watches it, no matter what the standard. Kids, Sunday pub football, the lot. My mum's only too pleased to get rid of him for a couple of hours! He never misses a Liverpool game, home or away. Wherever Jamie's playing, my dad's there watching. Jamie meets him after the game, takes him to the station, gets him his paper and sees him off on the train. He looks forward to that all week.

Given that influence it was no surprise that I should excel at football. I played for East London Schoolboys, right through from under-11s, and at that time East London Boys always had a reputation for being very good sides. I know many people think I'm steeped in West Ham tradition but when I was a kid, my old man and I were avid Arsenal fans. Jimmy Bloomfield was my big idol. Late in his career Jimmy signed for West Ham while I was a youngster there. The then manager Ron Greenwood, knowing how much I idolized Jimmy, rang me at home one morning.

'Get down to the ground, Harry,' he said. 'There's someone I want you to meet.' Lo and behold it's Jimmy. That was a moment to remember, meeting my idol.

In my early years at West Ham the dressing room was full of gamblers. Budgie Byrne and Alan Sealey were probably the biggest. It was a ritual the evening before a Saturday match to spend the night at the dogs. When we played away, wherever it was we went to the dogs. If it was Newcastle we'd go to Gosforth Park, if it was Manchester United or City we'd go to Salford, that's how it was. On the team coach the cards were always out. If we weren't playing we were gambling. That's the environment I joined when I first went to West Ham and in truth it helped me tremendously. I was a lot younger than the established players but they all liked me because I would join in their card games or their dog nights. I was one of the lads. Gambling helped me become accepted far more quickly than I could ever have hoped.

But I was never a serious gambler, and I'm still not. By that I mean I don't bet stupid money. I met Sandra when I was 17 and despite the reservations of her parents I really was saving up to buy a house. I suppose it's typical of life as a punter that my biggest-ever win was just over £8,000 – and to this day I haven't been paid out.

It was back in 1984 while I was Bournemouth manager and was asked to open a new betting shop in the town. I did it as a favour, despite the owner, who I knew quite well, offering me £200. Soon afterwards I was contacted by Alan Argeban, a mate of mine from Bournemouth. Alan is a terrific judge of the racing game. He knows all the jockeys and trainers and has things pretty well sorted out. He gave me six horses, all fancied, and I backed them all in doubles and trebles with this bookie whose shop I'd opened. Five won and the sixth was 10 lengths clear going to the last, clouted the hurdle, nearly threw his jockey off, but was still only beaten by a short-head in a photo-finish. God knows what the bet would have paid had all six won, but five winners paid £4,500. That was on the Saturday. On the Monday I rang the bookie and asked, with genuine concern, whether he'd had the chance to lay any of the bet off (for non-gamblers that means having the same bet to a smaller stake with a different bookie to lessen liabilities).

'No, I never,' he said.

'Gor blimey, that's hard lines,' I said. 'Only I've got another five horses today and they're all fancied as well.'

I think against his better judgement he laid the bet and, sure enough, all five copped for another £4,000 pay-out. Happy days for me. Or so I thought. When I phoned up the bookie after this latest success his reaction instantly sounded the alarm bells.

'You owe me eight and a half grand,' I said, perhaps a little ruthlessly.

'Err, would you fancy being a partner?' he asked, more than a little sheepishly.

'No. I don't want to be a partner, I just want my dough.'

He admitted he couldn't afford to pay me. He sent me the odd £50 every now and again but before too long the business went belly-up and I never got my dough after all.

But that didn't put me off horseracing. A few years later a group of about eight of us at Bournemouth put in a grand apiece to buy two horses. One was Slick Cherry, trained by David Elsworth, the other Up The Cherries, which went to Charlie Brooks. Up The Cherries was a big disappointment because Charlie had big hopes for it. It had one run on the all-weather at Lingfield, got injured and never ran again. We made a big loss on that. We had paid eight grand for it, but ended up with only £450 at auction after expenses. That wasn't a clever one, but Slick Cherry more than made up for it. Even if Slick Cherry had flopped, too, I would never have regretted going into racehorse ownership. It was a dream come true. I always think what my old nan would have said, from those days of being carted away by the police for operating as a bookie's runner in the back streets of East London, to her grandson owning a racehorse, just like all the toffs.

Slick Cherry won three times at Windsor, Chepstow, and Wincanton and what enjoyment it gave us those days. When it won its first race at Windsor, in 1990, I was still in hospital recovering from the car crash in Italy. The rest of the lads got me 14–1 for it and I listened to the commentary on the telephone. I think that helped speed my recovery. Then we went to Chepstow the following season and a couple of days before the race, trainer Elsworth said to me: 'Your horse has been working unbelievably well.' Apparently it had been working alongside Mountain Kingdom, which was a highly-rated Group horse. 'Your little filly has been walking all over Mountain Kingdom,' he went on. 'She's absolutely flying. I can't believe it.' There was a choice of two engagements for Slick Cherry, Chepstow on the Saturday or Windsor on the Monday.

'Where do you think we've got the best chance?' I asked Elsworth.

'It doesn't matter,' he said. 'This horse can't get beat. I know, we'll go to Chepstow. That way we'll get our money quicker.'

It was in the last race at Chepstow on the Saturday and Elsworth, famous as the man who trained the great Desert Orchid, had gone something like 48 days without a winner. Suddenly his bottle had gone. From being supremely confident, the nearer we got to the race the more his optimism ebbed away. I'd had a very big bet on Slick Cherry – a few hundred quid, which was far more than I would normally gamble – and

Elsworth's edginess was getting to us all. This wasn't how we had planned it.

'What's the matter, David?' I asked nervously, desperately hoping that this was his normal behaviour before a race.

'I don't know,' he said, staring glumly at the racecard. 'This one's fancied, and that one too, and I've just been speaking to so and so, and he fancies his…'

This was not what we wanted to hear. 'Well, what do you reckon?' I asked, almost pleadingly.

There was a pause. A group of us shot nervous glances at each other, recognizing all too clearly that we'd done our dough.

Elsworth continued to look at the floor. Finally: 'It's got to win. It's flying. It's got to win.' He was trying to convince himself, I think, more than us. He failed on both counts.

Slick Cherry ran that day. Very, very fast. She was 7–1, but won like an odds-on chance. Hands and heels. Never threatened. Me and Elsworth spent the next five minutes doing high fives. We kept running towards one another like a pair of nutters slapping our hands in the air. It's a wonder we weren't arrested.

Days like that are special. It's why I love racing so much, but I've got no ambitions to follow ex-England footballers Mike Channon or Francis Lee into the sport full time. I go racing about once a month and I love the atmosphere. Newbury, Wincanton and Fontwell are my favourite tracks. I'll walk around, have a bet, enjoy a bowl of eels or a curry in the winter. It's a great game, so long as it doesn't take over your life. You need something outside football because – there are no two ways about it – football really does take over your life. You need something else, which is why I've also started playing golf. Look at Alex Ferguson. He's got his hands full managing Manchester United but he's into racing in a big way. He owns a lovely little horse called Queensland Star which won on its first two outings and then ran at Royal Ascot. I suppose that's the difference in a nutshell between the Manchester Uniteds of this world and the West Hams. Fergie dabbles in Royal Ascot circles, I'm stuck at Wincanton.

Like me Fergie loves a bet, and like me he has an account with a firm called Surrey Racing, who invite the two of us every year to their box at Kempton. I remember one occasion when I rang up to place a bet and just before I put the phone down the telephonist said: 'Thank you very much, Mr Ferguson.' I'd given her my account number, which is only one digit different from Fergie's, and she had clearly chalked up the bet to the wrong account. Now, this was like something from a game of scruples. If the bet lost I could just keep quiet and Fergie would end up paying for it; if it won I could phone up and tell Surrey they'd made a mistake and I'd get my dough. I'm ashamed to admit I chickened out and pointed out the error straight away. You owe me one, Fergie!

I was fortunate enough during the 1997–98 season to pen a football tipping column in the *Racing Post*. I didn't do it for the money – you'd only have to look at the monthly cheque for proof of that. I did it because it made a refreshing change from talking to the press about injuries, transfers and the like. Football and betting are two of the great loves of my life, and there I was writing about both in the same column. It was a bit of fun and judging by the response it got I think an awful lot of people enjoyed reading it. I managed to tip a few winners, so much so that I got a bit cheeky and challenged the paper's No 1 tipster, Henry Rix, to a straight head-to-head at the Aintree Grand National meeting. Henry's a terrific judge, no doubt about that, but I managed to get a few whispers from Tony McCoy, the greatest jockey around, and going into the Saturday there was abolutely nothing between us. Neither of us tipped the Grand National winner Earth Summit, but there running on gallantly through the mud to get into fourth place was my each-way selection St Mellion Fairway, and that was enough to give me the edge over Henry. Two days later I found out Henry had suddenly left the *Post*. I hope it wasn't out of embarrassment.

CHAPTER 11

Life in the Hot Seat

Given the demands of life in the Premiership and the pressure it puts on managers it may come as a surprise to learn that the bosses of all the top-flight clubs get along famously. I know on occasions angry words are exchanged in the heat of the moment. I'm thinking here of the famous clashes between Kenny Dalglish and Alex Ferguson and the Kevin Keegan spat with Fergie when Newcastle and Manchester United were going hammer and tongs for the title in 1996. But once the dust has settled it's usually all friends again. Indeed many will have noticed that though the press like to pretend Kenny and Alex are bitter rivals, it was Alex who wrote the foreword to Kenny's recent autobiography. I can honestly say there is not one manager in the Premiership who I don't get along with. I suppose you could say it's like an exclusive brotherhood. We each recognize the strains and stresses we all operate under, and we all respect one another's abilities.

One of my favourite managers, who's currently in the role

of TV pundit, is Ron Atkinson, who has had the most colourful of careers in the various hot-seats he's occupied. I've always liked Ron. He's a real larger-than-life character and I find him great company. I remember taking West Ham to Coventry for Big Ron's first game in charge, and after handing the teamsheets into the referee's room about an hour before the kick-off, Ron invited me into his office. Both clubs were staring relegation in the face, but no one had told Ron. When he went to his fridge to pour us a drink it was empty, absolutely nothing in it. The next minute he was on the phone to his secretary.

'Look, I ordered six bottles of pink champagne and six red wine and they're not here. I've got the manager of West Ham here with me and I think you'll find I haven't signed my contract, so be quick.'

The girl came back and said something like: 'Do you always drink pink champagne, Mr Atkinson?'

'Do they make it in any other colour?' he said, winking at me. He was making jokes and all I could think about was how we were going to mark Peter Ndlovu.

That little exchange summed Ron up perfectly. He likes the high life. A real bubbly character and the game needs people like him.

I'm told he used to go into training at Coventry and each morning in the five-a-sides he'd pretend to be a different player. 'I'm John Barnes today,' he'd say, or 'I'm Maradona now.' One day he turned in after a heavy night the previous evening, looking particularly rough and with a splitting headache. 'I'm David Rennie today,' he said.

During his spell at Aston Villa, I remember Ron telling me he had a major fall-out with the wife of his Aston Villa defender, Shaun Teale, whom he'd signed from me at Bournemouth. I could sympathize with Ron on this one because the same lady once almost ran me over in a fit of rage. I know David Unsworth took some stick when his move from West Ham to

Villa Park was scuppered by his wife, and Mrs Teale was similarly protective of her husband.

Shaun did superbly when he arrived at Bournemouth from Weymouth, so much so that within weeks we had to rip up his contract and give him another, more lucrative, one. A couple of months later, with Shaun improving in leaps and bounds, we had to do the same again because he really was different class. The only snag was that Brian Tiler, managing director of Bournemouth, was on holiday at the time and we needed his signature to rubber-stamp the deal. By the time Brian returned, the contract was no longer valid because it had missed an important deadline. All that meant was that by the time we drew up a new one, Shaun would be out of pocket by something like £100. 'Don't worry about it,' Brian told me. 'He's been in the club house, rent free, five months longer than he should have been so he's well ahead of the game.'

A couple of days later I was heading for my office after training when I saw Mrs Teale hurrying away. I caught up with her in the car park and asked if everything was okay.

'You'll see if everything's okay when you get to your office,' she said.

'Why, what's the matter?' I asked.

'There's a letter on your desk, that's what,' she said. 'You've promised Shaun all sorts but you've been robbing him blind.'

'Leave off,' I said. 'It's only a hundred quid. You've had the club house for nothing for five months.'

This didn't pacify her. In fact quite the opposite and she gave me a mouthful.

'Do me a favour,' I said, 'Get in the car, piss off and do the washing up at home where you belong.'

By now she was in the car and seeing red. The engine burst into life and she reversed so fast, not realizing I was behind the car, that I had to jump out of the way, otherwise I'd probably still be lying in the car park at Dean Court. Mrs Teale certainly took a keen interest in her husband's welfare because she had similar fall-outs with Big Ron, who actually paid £500,000 for Tealey without even seeing him. Ron will say that he watched Teale, who was a superb signing for Villa, several times and that he knew he'd make it to the top, but deep down he knows he bought him purely on my recommendation.

Sandra and I were in Majorca on holiday when we bumped into Ron. Over a drink he asked me: 'Tell me Harry, who's the best centre half in the lower divisions?'

'Shaun Teale,' I said.

'Who does he play for?'

'He plays for me at Bournemouth.'

'Oh be serious,' Ron said. 'Forget Bournemouth. Tell me who's the best centre half.'

'Shaun Teale,' I repeated. 'He's different class.'

Ron didn't say anything else but later that night when we were in another bar, enjoying a bit of a dance and a sing-song, he resumed the Teale conversation.

'Is he really that good?' he asked me.

I told Ron that indeed he was and listed his different strengths, not mentioning any weaknesses because I honestly didn't think he had any. Next minute Ron's wife Maggie said: 'Do you know what, Ron? I believe Harry.' Ron nodded at me and said he'd give me a ring when we all got back to England.

A couple of weeks later Ron rang me at Bournemouth. 'Everything you said about Teale has been confirmed,' he said. 'The only thing is, a good judge has told me he's short of pace.'

'Well he ain't a good judge,' I said, 'because Tealey's as quick as lightning.'

'That'll do me,' Ron said. 'How much?'

And so we sold Teale for £500,000 to Aston Villa, where he became one of the best defenders in the country. But his wife didn't see eye to eye with Ron and when he left Villa I heard she rang the local radio station to air her strong opinions. A tough-minded lady indeed.

Kenny Dalglish has an unfortunate reputation with the press

and rival supporters but everyone in the game likes Kenny. I go back a long way with him. I remember at West Ham years ago when I was about 19, Kenny came for a two-week trial as a 14-year-old when he was almost certainly the best schoolboy footballer in Great Britain. Everyone wanted to sign him. I used to pick him up from his digs and take him to training and I liked him a lot. One Saturday morning Ron Greenwood arranged a practice match between the first team and the reserves and picked Kenny to play with the first team. As a 14-year-old. He scored the kind of typical Dalglish goal he was to become famous for, shielding the ball close to his body with his back to goal before turning and curling in a shot high into the far corner. Nobody could believe it. Ron said he'd give anything to sign him but he knew there was little hope. Every club in the country was chasing him. Years later when I negotiated with Kenny the sale of Jamie from Bournemouth to Liverpool, he remembered everybody's names, even kids he'd known only for those two weeks and who never even went on to make the grade. He had a fantastic memory. I like to think that because of our friendship all those years earlier, he took extra-special care of Jamie when he signed for Liverpool as a 17-year-old. I know he resigned soon after Jamie's arrival but in that short space of time he acted as a father figure to him, inviting him round to his home for Sunday lunch, taking him out for a game of golf, that sort of thing.

I suppose I should be sore at Kenny for stealing John Barnes and Stuart Pearce from right under my nose at the beginning of the 1997–98 season. They were both on their way on free transfers to Upton Park but right at the last moment Kenny swooped in and swept them away to Newcastle. Pearce is a great player, a true competitor and a real leader and he would have been a terrific signing for West Ham. I knew I had youngsters like Rio Ferdinand and Frank Lampard coming through and I thought Pearcey would be a great influence on them. I spoke to Dave Bassett, Pearce's manager at Forest and a good mate of mine, and he told me that I could have Stuart on a free, but not right away. 'He's a big hero here,' said Dave. 'I can't take over as manager and right away get rid of Pearcey. They'd lynch me.' But Dave told me that Stuart did want to leave. He'd been player-manager for a short spell and it would have been hard for him to go back to being just a player again. I think Dave also wanted Stuart to initiate the transfer. A couple of days later Dave rang me and told me Pearcey was available on a free. Unfortunately before I had the chance to fix up a meeting with him, news of his availability leaked out. Forest were playing a first-team match behind closed doors at Villa Park and one or two players asked where Pearcey was. Dave wasn't there either but one of his assistants let the cat out of the bag. The news spread like wildfire and within a couple of hours Kenny was on the phone to Pearcey. Newcastle had the lure of playing in the Champions League and I think Pearce at that stage of his career found such a carrot hard to resist.

It was a similar story with John Barnes. Jamie rang me and told me Barnesey was getting a free. He was left out of the Liverpool side for the first game of the season at Wimbledon and that night, after I'd returned from Barnsley where we got off to a flyer, I fixed up a meeting with him at a hotel in London. He agreed a deal with us but to be fair he'd rushed into it a little and hadn't really explored all his options. At that time no one else knew he was available on a free, and I knew that once such news broke everybody would be after him. I've always rated John Barnes very highly. He's a terrific footballer who plays the game the way I like to see it played. He's also a voice on the pitch and I thought that he, like Pearce, would be a great influence in the dressing room. We shook hands and I thought everything was okay. Within a couple of days, John had received calls from Manchester United and Spurs but said our deal was still on because we had shaken hands. Then later that day Kenny contacted him and I think it was then that John changed his mind. He was very apologetic, but I told him that he had to do what he thought was best. I didn't want him coming to West Ham if he would have felt happier elsewhere. Anyway he met Kenny and they offered him more money – although I must say we'd offered a good deal too – and he was turned on by the prospect of a crack at the Champions League.

I was upset at the time and I made some comments that perhaps were a little over the top. I said something about feeling let down by both Kenny and John, that it was bad form on their part the way they'd behaved. But that was disappointment getting the better of me. There are no hard feelings between me and John, Kenny, or Stuart. In fact I've probably got the hump more with Kenny for getting no thanks when we held Manchester United to a 1–1 draw on the last day of the 1994–95 season, a result which handed the title to Kenny's Blackburn Rovers. 'You watch,' I said to the lads, 'we'll get a crate of champagne in the post for this.' But not a bloody thing. He doesn't like spending his dough, does Kenny. Those Scots have earned their reputation. The least Blackburn chairman Jack Walker could have done was buy us a couple of players.

It was a real shock when Kenny left Newcastle at the start of the 1998–99 season. But he'll be back before too long. He's got too much to offer. How could Newcastle allow him to buy eight or nine players at the start of the season and then get rid of him after just two games? That was out of order. I think a couple of the directors, the ones disgraced in those newspaper reports in 1998, wanted to take the pressure off themselves when they returned and thought that by getting shot of Kenny – who wasn't popular with the fans – they could worm their way back into the supporters' good books.

Alex Ferguson and I have a lot in common. I wouldn't say we're best mates, but I do enjoy his company. He's a dedicated football man but he's able to enjoy his life outside the game and one of his passions is racing. We share a love of the sport. And betting too. When we meet we have a chat about who we fancy for the championship, what the best odds are, maybe the day's best bets on the football coupon, even though of course we are no longer allowed to bet on our own sport following Sir John Smith's report. I've got a lot of respect for Alex, whose record in football is second to none.

Dave Bassett, who has steered Forest back into the Premiership, is another manager I get on particularly well with. We're very similar characters. Like me he's a Londoner, like me he's down to earth, and I think he's great company. Dave was with Frank Lampard and me on the day Slick Cherry won at Chepstow in 1991. He'd planned to spend the weekend in Bournemouth but we dragged him to the races. Dave had never had a bet in his life but stuck £100 on Slick Cherry. That was the first of his results. I'd booked him into a hotel in Bournemouth and the gaffer there didn't charge him. Then that night he came along to my restaurant in Bournemouth and had a big slap-up meal, with me and Frank Lampard paying the bill because we'd won so much at the races. 'I'll come back here again,' he said.

Dave effs and blinds like there's no tomorrow. I remember during another night at the restaurant every other word out of his mouth was an expletive. We weren't drinking or being rowdy, that's just the way Dave is. Anyway on the very next table was a local solicitor and his wife, well within earshot of Dave in full flow.

'Dave,' I whispered, nodding to the other couple. 'Keep the swearing down a bit.'

'Oh sorry, Harry,' he said and kept his language clean – for at least 30 seconds. Next minute it was f****** this and f****** that and the solicitor and his missus stood it for only another five minutes before walking out. 'Oh no,' I thought. 'He's ruining my business.'

When I was manager of Bournemouth Dave came on wanting to sign one of my players, someone I was anxious to get rid of. But I told Dave not to sign him. I'd have sold him to most other managers but not Dave. I didn't want to sell him a wrong 'un and I think he appreciated that. But Dave is massively enthusiastic and his record of getting teams promoted speaks for itself.

Joe Kinnear at Wimbledon is another character, too. Joe's another guy who loves his racing. He likes nothing better than a night out at Walthamstow dogs, where I think he has a couple of greyhounds in training, and you've got to admire what he's done at Wimbledon. But I must admit I was seriously disappointed in Joe's behaviour during the 1996–97 season when West Ham were really struggling. It was just before we signed Hartson and Kitson and I was searching desperately for a striker. I wanted to buy Dean Holdsworth from Wimbledon and I'm not exaggerating when I say I must have made 70 calls trying to track Joe down. I phoned the training ground, Selhurst Park, his home, I left messages on his answerphone and still he wouldn't get back to me. Now that's totally out of order. I don't care who rings me, it could be the manager of the lowliest non-League club but I will always return his call. It's common courtesy. I found it very hard to understand why Joe was acting that way. Eventually Frank Lampard managed to fix up a meeting at a Chinese restaurant near Joe's Mill Hill home. When I asked him why he was playing the Scarlet Pimpernel he didn't have an answer, just some lame excuse that he'd been busy. I told him of my interest in Holdsworth and he replied that Holdsworth didn't figure in his plans, that he did want to offload the striker, and that he'd speak to his chairman Sam Hammam.

'Ring me tomorrow,' he said.

Next day same story. I just couldn't get hold of him. His secretary would say she was just putting me through and then suddenly come back and say Joe had just left. A week went by before we had any further contact with Wimbledon, a week with relegation looking increasingly inevitable. Finally, the phone rang and it was Sam Hammam.

'If you want Holdsworth you'll have to give us £5 million plus Rio Ferdinand,' he said.

The conversation went no further. Instead we bought Hartson and Kitson and the rest is history. It was an altogether unsavoury episode and I remember thinking even during those blackest of times: 'Every dog has his day, Joe.' The following season we sold Michael Hughes to Wimbledon and I suppose I could have played silly buggers like Joe to get my own back, but I wouldn't stoop so low.

Soon after that incident, with Hartson and Kitson in the side, we drew 1–1 at Wimbledon towards the end of the season when we needed every point we could get to survive. In the press conference shortly afterwards Joe told reporters: 'I really do hope West Ham stay up – they're normally good for six points every season.' Very funny, Joe. Perhaps it's the right time to point out that last season we did the double over Wimbledon. I could gloat, Kinnear-like, but that's not my style. Having said that, the joke was on me in September 1998 when Wimbledon came from 3–0 down to beat us 4–3 at Upton Park.

Another of the managers I really like is Roy Evans at Liverpool. He's a smashing feller. And I'm looking forward to renewing my acquaintance with Walter Smith, the new manager of Everton. I bumped into Walter in Bermuda a couple of years ago and I found him terrific company. He had a great record at Rangers and I think given time he'll do well at Goodison. Jim Smith at Derby is great fun too. I enjoy a night with Smithy, and I think he's forgiven me for stealing Paolo Futre from under his nose. Win or lose, Jim will have you in his office after the game with a couple of bottles of red wine.

A bottle of red wine is my preferred tipple on a Saturday night. Regardless of the result, Sandra and I will go out Saturday nights, most often with Frank Lampard and his wife Pat, Sandra's sister. Frank is my brother-in-law but he's also my best mate. We'll generally go to Lorenzo's, my restaurant in Bournemouth. It's an interest I've had for about 10 years now and it does okay, but I've no intention of starting a chain of Planet Redknapps. I'm far too busy with the football to get too involved. I leave the running of it to Lorenzo, a former waiter who first approached me with the idea of buying it.

Saturday night I class as the end of my working week, the time for me to wind down. I couldn't sit at home after a bad defeat moping around. That would do me in. We always go out and after that first bottle of red wine even the heaviest defeat does not seem quite so painful. I don't go back to the training ground until Monday but from Sunday football is very much top of the agenda again. If things haven't gone well the day before I have no urge to read the newspapers but if we've had a good win I'll buy them all. And of course on Sundays during the season there are always games on TV and I make sure I watch them. If a live TV game involves a team we are due to meet shortly, I travel to the game to watch it there rather than on TV. And I'll always be at a Liverpool game on a Sunday to watch Jamie play. The rest of the working week is spent training and watching games, although I'll always do my best to take Sandra out on Thursdays when there are rarely any matches.

I suppose looking at the anxious faces of managers during a Premiership clash you'd find it hard to imagine that we can find the time to relax on a match day, but we always manage a half-hour or so to forget about the pressures. The normal routine for an away match, say at Old Trafford, is to travel up to Manchester on the Friday night. On the Saturday morning Frank and I and a few of the staff will go for a walk before getting the players up for a few stretching exercises. We'll all have a pre-match meal at around noon, but the food the players eat nowadays is vastly different to the grub served up when I was starring for West Ham in the Sixties. In the old days it was fillet steak and rice pudding, probably the worst thing you could eat because it would lay on your stomach for hours. Nowadays they eat cereals or pasta, food high in carbo-hydrates, and water has replaced the gallons of tea we used to drink. We'll get to the ground at about 1.30pm and I'll hold a team talk after first announcing my starting XI. But the players will already know by then what the team is because I'll have worked on set-pieces in training. Some managers won't name their team until an hour before the kick-off and their players won't have a clue who's starting. The team-sheets have to be given to the referee by 2pm so Fergie and I would go together to the ref's room. Then there is an hour of hanging about before the match. You can't spend all that time in the dressing room. I like to get out of the dressing room and leave the players to it, maybe returning about 20 minutes before the kick-off to gee them up a bit. That's what most managers do. I'd go into Fergie's office for half an hour or so, have a cup of tea, exchange a bit of small talk. After the game and the obligatory press conference, the home manager invites you and your staff for a couple of glasses of wine while the players are getting changed, and then it's onto the coach for the drive home. I can honestly say that no matter what has happened on the pitch, I've never had a bust-up with a rival manager once the final whistle has gone.

Many fans have asked me what makes the ideal manager and I think it's a difficult question to answer. You've got to have enthusiasm and you have to be a good judge of a player. They are the two most important factors. If you buy more bad players than good, then you won't last long in the job. And you've got to have the knack of knowing how to handle players. Some of them need to be criticized, others molly-coddled. I have a very relaxed atmosphere with the players but they know I can turn at any moment. It's important to have your own individual style. You can't copy anyone or you'll soon get found out. You have to have your own personality and if that's good enough for you to do the job then fine. If not then you'd better look for alternative employment. You should not try to be someone you're not.

Of course we all make mistakes and we all regret things we might have said or done. For instance during the 1997–98 season I ripped into our keeper Ludo Miklosko after he gave away two silly goals against Derby. For one of the goals he tried to chip the ball out to the wing but succeeded only in passing to their centre forward. In the press conference afterwards I was asked what I said to Miklosko in the dressing room. 'Oh I just said next time make sure your chip over the centre forward is a little higher,' I said sarcastically. 'What do you think I said? He made two f****** cock-ups and they cost us the game. He's paid not to make mistakes.' In the papers the next day it was all about Redknapp going on the warpath at Miklosko and Ludo took it very personally. Some players would have accepted the rap but Ludo is a bit more sensitive and I should have handled things differently. That's the way I am, though. I say what's on my mind. I upset John Hartson for saying he was an idiot to get sent off against Derby, in the corresponding fixture. But that's what I felt. He was an idiot. He punched Igor Stimac, possibly a payback for what happened on his West Ham debut, and deserved to be sent off. I couldn't pretend John was unlucky. I had to tell it like it was. At the same time I'm quick to shower acclaim on a player if I think he merits it. It's no use John accepting the plaudits and then getting the hump whenever flak flies his way.

I've never been one of those managers who throws teacups around the dressing room, but there was one occasion when the performance of one of my players really did annoy me, and didn't he pay a price! We were at Southampton towards the end of the 1994–95 season and were drawing 1–1 with two minutes to go. Don Hutchison was stood on the halfway line, hands on hips, when the feller he was with started running with the ball. He ran all the way into our box while Hutch stood there looking at him, not moving an inch. He could have cost us the game. I wasn't happy with him afterwards, but in the dressing room he wouldn't accept what I was saying and kept making smart-arse excuses. In the end I lost my temper and threw a plate of sandwiches over his head. What a sight, egg, cheese and tomato right across the nut. That's when management is definitely not good for your health.

So much has changed during my career as a manager, perhaps nothing more so than the way transfer deals are conducted. Years ago if you fancied a player you'd just ring his manager and come to some sort of arrangement. Simple as that. But now it's all done through agents. All tip-offs. They'll ring you and tell you a player is unsettled at a club and is looking for a transfer and will go on to say how much the player is looking for in wages and so on. I know most fans think agents are frowned upon by those of us inside football, but nowadays they are an integral part of a transfer. Most managers are happy to negotiate with agents because they recognize them as a necessary evil. For instance the moment I ring a manager and tell him I'm releasing one of my players, the value automatically goes down. But if an agent puts the word around, something like 'I hear West Ham may be prepared to sell so and so. I don't think they want to lose him but I hear he's desperate to get away,' then the asking price will remain at the level you want it. Many fans are puzzled why top-class players nearing the end of their careers – players like Ian Wright, John Barnes and Stuart Pearce – are allowed to leave a club on a free transfer or next to nothing when they are still well capable of commanding a decent fee. But granting a player a free transfer is recognition of the service they've given to the club. It means the buying club, through not having to pay a fee, are able to afford better wages. I suppose in a way it's an alternative to granting a testimonial. Of course at a Premiership club it's not just the manager who gets involved in transfer deals.

At West Ham managing director Peter Storrie plays his part. He's great to work with and I have a very similar relationship with him to the one I enjoyed with Brian Tiler at Bournemouth. When I approach him and say there's a player I want to buy, he will have a word with the chairman and if the two of them say the club can afford the price, then we'll move in. Neither Peter nor the chairman would ever come back and say they don't fancy the player. That's not their job. That's my job and they back my judgement. Peter has been a terrific help to me since I've been at West Ham. And I also have a lot of time for my chairman, Terry Brown. He has a genuine love for the club and he stood by me when things were at their bleakest during those grim days early in 1997 when other chairmen would perhaps have changed their manager.

I have been disturbed over the last couple of years to see that while salaries for players have sky-rocketed, managers' pay has nowhere near kept pace. The influx of foreign players led to an increase in wages throughout the Premiership, but us bosses could not book a ticket on the gravy train. Suddenly I found I was getting less than my most ordinary player and that can't be right. If you're manager of a Premiership club you've got massive responsibilities. If things don't go well you're out, and that could be the end of your career. I felt that the likes of myself, Jim Smith, Dave Bassett, managers who'd been around the block, were not getting the rewards we deserved. We were established managers yet our salaries were static while foreign coaches coming into the game were getting vast wages.

At the risk of sounding arrogant, when you're managing a Premiership club you're at the top of your profession. There are only 20 of us. You could almost say we're the chosen few. It's criminal therefore that we could be earning less than a player not even guaranteed a place in the first team. Something needed to be done and I'm glad to say that recently our lot has improved. But it has still a lot further to go before I'm completely happy. Given the responsibility I must shoulder, the constant pressure I'm under, surely my pay should be on a par with my top players.

It's the same with the amount of money at managers' disposal. There are a lot of good managers who get written off because they haven't got the players and can't afford to buy them. These foreign coaches are coming in and I'm sure some of them are bringing in good ideas but they've got a head start going to big clubs. If they are such great coaches let them turn a team like Barnsley into top-six material in the Premiership. Ruud Gullit was a fantastic player and I'm sure he's a good coach, but he was given a hell of a chance at Chelsea with an open cheque-book. He now has another chance at Newcastle. The same with Luca Vialli.

People say so-and-so is a great manager because his team are at the top, but is he really? Is Alex Ferguson that much cleverer than, say, George Burley at Ipswich or is the difference down to the fact he has so much dough to spend? If you've got the dough you've got more of a chance. I know you've got to spend it right but if I said to someone 'here's £15 million to spend' he could probably go out and buy four good players. You don't have to be a managerial genius to know that buying Alan Shearer would make a team better. I don't think buying a team is that difficult. It's when you haven't got money that it's really hard. You're always taking chances, gambling on players and wondering if they're really good enough. My chairman once said to me: 'You can't buy success, Harry.' I told him that was a load of bollocks. 'Have a look at the League table,' I said. 'The teams at the top are the ones with money.'

I hope I'm not giving the impression that I'm unhappy in my job. Far from it. I make a good living from it. Managing West Ham United has afforded me a pleasant lifestyle. There's nothing like the buzz I get on a Saturday night after a good win. It's a fantastic feeling. And I love to see youth players develop into fully-fledged first-team performers. That gives me an awful lot of satisfaction. But the downs are tough. When you are struggling, when fans are sitting there hurling abuse at you, that ain't a lot of fun. People think you get beaten, you go home in your big car and that's the end of it. But that's so far wide of the mark. If we lose on a Saturday my weekend is absolutely ruined. I don't recover until a Monday morning when I walk into my office at our training ground at Chadwell Heath. I have to pick myself up then because I have to lift the players. But you should see me on a Saturday night or all day Sunday after a

Left: West Ham managing director, Peter Storrie, has been a great help to me at Upton Park.

Above: West Ham chairman Terence Brown – refused to accept my resignation when Hammers looked doomed in the winter of 1997.

Left: Racehorse owner, Michael Tabor, who so nearly took control of West Ham, celebrates after winning the 2000 Guineas in 1997 with Entrepreneur.

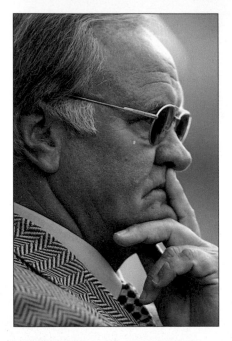

Left: Big Ron Atkinson – one of my favourite Premiership managers because he's always obliging with the pink champagne!

Below: Making a point. In familiar pose, in March 1997, in the thick of West Ham's relegation battle.

Above: Kenny Dalglish, the former Newcastle manager, stole John Barnes and Stuart Pearce from under my nose.

Right: Terry Venables. He took his revenge after failing to sign Jamie for Spurs.

'*You wouldn't like me when I'm angry…*' *Referee, David Elleray and Spurs defender, Colin Calderwood, feel the Redknapp wrath.*

Bournemouth reach the dizzy heights of Division Two for the first time in their history (1986–87) – reason enough to celebrate with my jubilant Cherries players.

Above: Me and my mate Brian Tiler during our Bournemouth days. I still miss him terribly.

Below: The tangled wreckage of our minibus, after the crash in Latina, which claimed Brian's life. It was a miracle any of us survived.

Harry tells of his brush with death

EXCLUSIVE
BY DENNIS LANDSBERT IN LATINA ITALY.

AFC Bournemouth manager Harry Redknapp's injuries are worse than originally believed.

He is suffering from a hairline fracture of the skull, a broken nose, cracked ribs and a severe gash to his left leg.

In an exclusive interview from his hospital bed in Latina, Harry told the Echo he remembers nothing about the crash itself.

Harry, 47, was dragged, unconscious and covered in petrol, from the twisted, mangled wreckage of the minibus.

"I had just dozed off when the accident happened and I woke up two days later in hospital," he said.

"The people who pulled me out thought I was dead," he added.

Harry has been told he will have to remain in hospital for at least a week before he can fly back home.

His two sons - Jamie, 17, and Mark, 20, - have flown out to Italy to be at their father's bedside.

Harry's wife Sandra is staying in England, reportedly on his instructions.

But Latina hospital staff and patients' families have also rallied round the injured English party,

The wreckage of the bus and the car involved in Sunday's fatal accident

vors, bringing flowers and fruit to their bedsides.

"Everyone has been magnificent - very, very kind. I have a top doctor looking after me," said Harry.

"My main worry is my leg, which has a terrible gash in it. But basically I'm just very glad to be alive."

"Doctors have told me I will have to rest up for quite a while, so that is what I will do.

"But after that I will be back to work. I don't expect I'll be putting a track suit on for some time though."

Harry was pulled from the minibus by York City FC chairman Michael Sinclair.

Mr Sinclair, 48, said he remembered hearing a terrible bang and the minibus seemed to somersault, before sliding 50 yards along the road.

Despite his injuries, Mr Sinclair

managed to drag all the survivors from the vehicle.

Brian Tiler's body is expected to be returned to England in a week's time.

● BRIAN TILER's body will flown home to England next week.

The delay is due to lengthy ministration between British Italian undertakers.

A funeral service will be held the Moordown Baptist Church

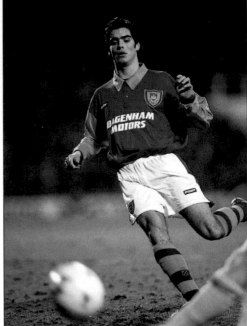

Above: Florin Raducioiu. The Romanian international was well named because his performances for us were worth about two bob!

Above: Dani, the Portugese playboy, was a big hit with the fans at Upton Park.

Below: Paolo Futre – got 'shirty' on his Hammers debut.

Below: Joey Beauchamp caused me nothing but aggravation from the very first day he signed. It was an immense relief to get rid of him.

Left: Hammers cult hero Julian Dicks. I wouldn't fancy knocking his pint over!

Above: Two for the top – that's Rio Ferdinand and Frank Lampard, products of the thriving youth scheme at West Ham.

Left: John Hartson and Paul Kitson celebrate a goal during our 5–1 win over Sheffield Wednesday in May 1997. Their goals helped save us from relegation that season.

The Wright stuff. I show off my big summer signing before the start of the 1998–99 season.

Above: My mate Bobby Moore at the height of the Bogota bracelet incident. No one was less likely than Bobby to be guilty of stealing.

Right: Frank Lampard and I share a joke in training. Frank has been a fantastic help to me at West Ham.

Below: My good pal Billy Bonds and I during happier days. I miss his friendship.

defeat. I'm not the best company. Problems stay on the mind morning, noon and night. I can't switch off, sometimes can't sleep at night, and can't talk to people because I don't know what they're saying. I'm not listening. I'm miles away. 'Great company you were last night,' Sandra will often say to me in a sarcastic tone. But I can't help it. How she puts up with it I don't know. But she does. When she sees me withdrawing into my own thoughts she'll let me get on with it. She won't interrupt. There's not much point if she did – I wouldn't hear her.

The 1996–97 season, when West Ham were really struggling and I offered to resign, was one of the blackest times of my life. The pressures affected my health. I remember trying to back the car out of my drive one morning but I couldn't turn around to look through the window because my neck was so sore through all the pressure and tension I was feeling. It gets to you. You don't want to be a failure. Having achieved what I still think was a minor miracle in keeping West Ham up the first season I took charge at the beginning of the 1994–95 campaign, it was hard to accept that we were going to end up in Division One after all. We finished 14th in the first season I took charge, five points clear of a relegation slot, but to this day I don't know how. We had a bad side and I had no money to spend. We weren't good enough to stay in the Premiership, no two ways about it. Finishing 14th that term was a better achievement than almost reaching Europe in 1997–98. I remember going to Farnborough Town, a non-League side, in our final pre-season match in 1994, and losing comprehensively even though I fielded my full first team. They were better than us, pure and simple as that, and I remember thinking that night that I wasn't going to enjoy the next nine months. But somehow we managed to get the best out of every player, to keep the confidence high, and somehow we scraped through. The pressures of a relegation scrap are enormous. It hurts your pride, your self-esteem. You want people to think you're good at your job and that's what it's all about. It's not about bonuses and money, it's about being good at your job, the pride you take in it, the pride you take from other people recognizing that you know what you're doing. I do believe I'm good at what I do but that season I could see everything crashing around my ears. If we had got relegated I was out of a job. I knew I'd look back on it and say to myself that I didn't have the tools to do the job, that I was saddled with a group of players not good enough to perform in the Premiership, but the only thing on record would be that West Ham were relegated and Harry Redknapp was manager at the time. You bear it all on your own shoulders and take it personally. It's all your fault.

And of course it affects your family. It was hard for Sandra. I remember we were due to go out to celebrate my birthday, in March 1997, but we'd just lost at Leeds to dump us right in the thick of the relegation zone. While I was sitting at a table in a restaurant I couldn't utter a word to Sandra. I was just like a zombie. Previously when we lost in the FA Cup to Wrexham, in January, I think Sandra wanted me to pack it in. She could see me feeling more and more down. It wasn't as if I was going home and having a row with her. It was just that I was miserable and I couldn't snap out of it and that's not like me. I was hurt. Hurt at the thought of being regarded as a failure. Hurt that the club was struggling so badly. Hurt that I didn't seem able to do anything about it.

And when you're down people like to put the boot in. One of the things that hurt me the most during those gloomy times was an article by Jimmy Greaves questioning the appointment of Frank Lampard as my assistant. Jimmy suggested that the move owed more to Frank being my brother-in-law than any footballing reasons and that wounded both Frank and I deeply. I idolized Jimmy Greaves as a kid and when he came to West Ham when I was there as a player I was delighted. He was the most fantastic goalscorer I've ever seen and the most terrific feller you could wish to meet. In his short time at Upton Park everybody loved Jimmy. I got on great with him, I still do. I enjoy watching him on TV and reading the stuff he writes for *The Sun*, but the comments he made in one of those articles really put the knife in, to an already wounded man. This is what he wrote:

'Bobby Moore, probably the greatest footballer this country ever produced, was once asked to select his favourite game. Not his most significant or his greatest. His favourite, the one he enjoyed the most. You are probably thinking you know the answer. And you would be wrong. Bobby did pick a Wembley final against some Germans, but it took place in 1965, not 1966. West Ham 2 Munich 1860 0.

'That was his favourite game, the night his club won the European Cup Winners' Cup. He said: "The team had all grown up together, we'd known each other for ever. It felt like winning the trophy with your school team."

'And looking back there is indeed something unique about that West Ham side. They might not be the only all-English team to triumph in Europe – Manchester City repeated the achievement in 1970 – but they are certainly the most local. Going through the names, nine were Londoners – six of those from within a mile or two of Upton Park – and only defender Joe Kirkup, a Geordie, and Geoff Hurst, from Ashton-under-Lyme, came from outside the capital. That was the tradition of West Ham. That is why they were called the Academy. Not because they always played wonderful football. But because after training, local men would sit in local cafes and discuss different ways of training, coaching and playing.

'Harry Redknapp, another local, will of course be aware of this history. Which is why it must hurt him deeply to have presided over a period that has seen the club lose its identity almost totally. I like Harry. Everybody does. I think that is why he has escaped a lot of the flak that would be thrown at other managers had they put their club in this position. Can you imagine for instance if Gerry Francis had bought Paolo Futre and tried to play him up front with Iain Dowie? Or had gone to court to get a work permit for Ilie Dumitrescu and then sold him at a loss less than a year later? Could you imagine it if Graeme Souness had bought two Romanian forwards to a club that couldn't score goals and never tried playing them up front together? Or sold Tony Cottee to Malaysia and then announced he didn't know where his next goal is coming from? And could you imagine it if, in appointing Arsene Wenger, Arsenal had managed to lose a hero like Pat Rice from the coaching staff? And when Wenger was asked who his right-hand man might be, he replied: "My brother-in-law"?

'Now think about the departure of Billy Bonds and the arrival of Frank Lampard at Upton Park. Of course Frank might be a tactical genius, and for West Ham's sake I hope he is. No doubt when Harry sits down to talk he can explain many of these decisions. And because I like the bloke and want him to succeed I would accept his reasoning. But isn't that what everyone has been doing lately? Giving Harry, his players, even the board of directors the benefit of the doubt.

'At least Harry had the decency to offer his resignation after losing 1–0 to Wrexham last week. That he is prepared to walk away if he thinks it would help the club is a sign that he still cares. If only the board were as selfless. Because what would certainly help Harry's decision-making is the swift injection of £30 million from Michael Tabor. And if, as the present Hammers board claim, there are "strings attached", then so there bloody well should be. Do these buffoons really believe a bloke gives over £30 million without a few conditions? "Here's £30 million, boys. Punt third favourites for a place at Kempton with it for all I care. I'm off down the pub."

'No, that is not how it happens. Tabor will want control, shares, flotation, repayment if he leaves, all the usual small print that protects every businessman who buys a football club, from Jack Walker to Alan Sugar and Sir John Hall. But he will give money for players and that is what West Ham need most desperately. Because it is exactly that cash shortage which has led to West Ham losing touch with their roots. They tried to play the big game with too little money.

'They wanted foreign internationals, but not ones like Gianfranco Zola or Fabrizio Ravanelli who might cost a few quid. So they got a half-crippled legend from Portugal, two Romanians of suspicious club pedigree, and a Dutchman who went potty and lived in a caravan. West Ham was not built on importing poseurs from around the world. The odd poseur from Plaistow, maybe, but it remained the most resolutely local of all clubs. That is what made it special, that is what helped it survive. I was born in Dagenham and I knew, even when I went to Chelsea, Spurs and Milan, that I would one day end up getting a game at Upton Park.

'The sad thing is, I probably still could.'

It was a hurtful article. I don't know how Jimmy ever came to the conclusion that Frank owed his job purely to his relationship with me. Frank had played at Upton Park for 20 years. It wasn't as if I was employing my brother-in-law from the local fish and chip shop. He knew the game inside out, and knew West Ham inside out. He had decided when he finished his playing career that he didn't want to move into coaching, but he still had a great love for the game, still watched a million games. When I asked him to join me he was happy to give up his interests outside the game and throw himself into the job full time. And that's exactly what he's done. He's been fantastic and I couldn't have been luckier than having Frank working with me. So Jimmy's criticism was very hurtful; when good friends give you stick so publicly it wounds you deeply.

One of the aspects of management that some bosses find wearisome but which I have largely enjoyed is dealing with the press. I have a pretty good relationship with most national football writers and I'll often go out of my way to help a pressman if I can. But you do find that some of them will stick the knife in to you the first chance they get. I had *Sun* reporter

Ben Bacon in my office several times, helping him out whenever I could. But then he wrote an article siding with Florin Raducioiu in which he absolutely slaughtered me. I booted him out of the training ground the next time I saw him. It made me realize that you can give some journalists all the help you can but they're still well capable of turning on you.

Regularly during the 1997–98 season I was employed by Sky or ITV as a studio analyst and I must say I enjoyed the experiences. I was going to the games anyway so there was no harm in helping the TV lads out, particularly as there was a few quid in it for me. I don't think I made any horrendous cock-ups, but one TV appearance I made years ago while manager of Bournemouth still makes me cringe whenever I think of it. It was just after we'd beaten Manchester United in the FA Cup, in January 1984. It was a sensational result for a small club like Bournemouth and I think I let the occasion get the better of me. I was a young manager just starting out and it was my first real taste of glory. I was wheeled out onto the pitch minutes after the final whistle and all the jubilant Bournemouth crowd were surrounding me. The interviewer asked me whether I felt sorry for Ron Atkinson, the United manager.

'No,' I said. 'Why should I feel sorry for him? I'd like to be earning what he'll be picking up this week.'

It was an incredibly graceless remark and when I saw it on TV later it made my toes curl with embarrassment. I had a taste of what Ron must have felt that day when we lost to Wrexham in the Cup in January 1997, and if Wrexham boss Brian Flynn had said similar things about me, he'd have gone down in my estimation. But luckily Ron has never held it against me.

Managers are obliged nowadays to appear live in front of the Sky TV cameras sometimes just minutes after the final whistle. You may have just suffered a calamitous defeat and no way do you want to go out and put on a smiling face, but now that's part of the job. It's easy for those people sitting cosily in the studio to analyse what's gone wrong. It annoys me when a rival manager sitting in the studio criticises the tactics you've used when his side has been stuffed the previous day. What about his own tactics? Get them right first. I don't mind them criticizing how the team has played because they have a right to their opinion, but they should not start bad-mouthing another manager's tactics.

As far as the players I've handled in my career goes, some have been real handfuls, others model pros. You have to take the rough with the smooth. But the only thing that really gets up my nose about players is when they put themselves above the punters. I've got no time for people who don't sign autographs for the kids or don't take time to have a chat with supporters. After all, they're the people who pay their wages. If supporters are well-mannered and want to talk to me, I'll talk to them, and I think players should be exactly the same. I like to think I get on well with the majority of West Ham fans. I think they feel I am on their wavelength. One of the things I changed when I became West Ham manager was to allow fans in to the training ground. When I first came they had to stand outside the gate and couldn't see anything, but now we invite them all in. And why not? If they're good enough to spare the time to come to our training sessions, we should play ball with them.

The players are not gods, after all. They're only football players. Big deal.

CHAPTER 12

The Bust-ups

There is no bigger admirer than me of the coaching abilities of former England manager, Terry Venables, but Tel has another side to his character as I found when I was still serving my managerial apprenticeship with Bournemouth.

Jamie was attached to Spurs from the age of 11 and signed schoolboy forms for them when he reached 14. Most of the big clubs in London were after him, Everton too, but for some reason he was always keen on Tottenham. He trained there occasionally but played local football in Bournemouth at the weekend. Soon after leaving school, however, he changed his mind and said he wasn't going. He'd decided to sign for me at Bournemouth instead. He didn't want to mess around for years in the youth team at White Hart Lane, he said. He wanted to play League football as soon as he could. I think his mind had been made up by Sean Murray, a schoolboy superstar and a friend of his at Spurs. Sean captained

England Schoolboys two years running, which believe me was no mean feat. But he was going nowhere at Tottenham. His career seemed to be going a bit stale and he warned Jamie against staying, telling him that Tottenham didn't give bright young players their chance. So Jamie was adamant that he wanted to join Bournemouth. To be honest, I wasn't keen on the idea. I knew by now he was going to be a player, a top player, and I believed he'd be better off with a top club, but he dug his heels in and wouldn't budge. The only guarantee he wanted from me was that I would pick him for the first team if I thought he was good enough. So I rang Terry at Tottenham and told him that Jamie wasn't going back to White Hart Lane. He wasn't best pleased. He said Spurs were signing 12 kids that year, and Jamie was the one they wanted above all. 'You and Jamie come up to see me', he said, no doubt hoping to change his mind.

We had a long chat with Terry, who told Jamie to go away and think about it, but there was nothing to think about. Jamie's mind was made up, he was staying at Bournemouth. When I informed Terry of his decision he turned nasty. He accused me of being slippery – a case of the pot calling the kettle black, I replied – and clearly believed I had influenced Jamie. We had a blazing row down the phone and fell out big time. Terry was smarting more and more about it and things were in danger of getting out of hand, so Brian Tiler stepped in as peacemaker without my knowledge. Brian agreed to pay 25 per cent of any transfer fee we received for Jamie, up to £300,000, with a further 10 per cent of anything above that, but when I found out what he'd agreed with the Spurs boss, I hit the roof.

'What?' I shouted. 'What have you done that for? Don't give them anything.' But Brian said the deal was done.

Yet that clearly didn't appease Mr Venables. Later that year, Christmas 1989 to be exact, Bournemouth were drawn away to Tottenham in the FA Youth Cup, a dream tie for the kids at my club. But shortly before the game a flu virus swept through the hostel where the kids had digs and they were all laid low. We couldn't raise a team. I rang Spurs to re-arrange another date and spoke to John Lyall, who had recently joined them as an assistant after his departure from the West Ham hot seat.

'No problem,' I was told. An hour later I got another call from Spurs. 'Sorry, we can't call the game off. You've got to play.' Clearly this was Terry's decision.

'But we can't raise a team,' I said.

Spurs reported us to the League who said that if we didn't fulfil the fixture, Spurs would go through. And that's what happened. They threw us out of the cup. I was really disappointed for the kids and I was disgusted with Spurs. There was no doubt in my mind this was an act of spite, pay-back for what had happened with Jamie. I told Spurs that we knew they would hammer us no matter when the tie was played so what difference did the date make. It wasn't as if I was trying to gain any advantage. But they just ignored my pleas. It was a terrible blow for the kids at Dean Court. They were never going to be top-class players but this was a chance in a lifetime for them to play at a League ground like White Hart Lane. How could Tottenham stoop so low?

Yet a few years later when Terry became manager of England, he held no grudges. He was only too pleased to pick Jamie and thought the world of him. I've spoken to him many times since and we have no problems. To be honest I think Terry Venables is the best coach in the business. When he concentrates on football, there is no one to touch him. He's more knowledgeable than anyone in the game, and he handles players superbly. When he was England boss he invited the managers of all the London Premiership clubs to a hotel in London for a meeting. Gerry Francis, Glenn Hoddle, Bruce Rioch and myself were there. He stood up and talked football for two hours, discussing at length the great

Ajax system, and he was so interesting. It was brilliant. He has a great personality and I know Jamie idolized him when he was in charge of the national team.

You can be sure that whenever West Ham fans get together to discuss the club's worst-ever signings, the name of Joey Beauchamp will figure prominently. He was trouble from the word go and to this day I'm convinced he played a key role in Billy Bonds' decision to quit West Ham. It was in the summer of 1994, just before I took over from Bill as manager, that we bought Beauchamp for £1 million from Oxford. We'd tried to sign him earlier but he'd turned us down and looking back I think we both realized we should have forgotten all about him there and then. But Bill and I both knew the lad could play and so we went back for him. If only we hadn't.

The first day of pre-season training Beauchamp walked up to me and said: 'I've made a mistake. I should have gone to Swindon.'

I genuinely thought he meant he'd driven the wrong way to the training ground and in all innocence replied: 'Why, did you come down the M4?'

He looked at me blankly and repeated: 'I should have gone to Swindon.'

'No,' I said. 'Swindon's the opposite direction…'

'I mean I should have signed for Swindon,' he said. 'This is too far from home.'

I couldn't believe it. Was this really happening? Here's a guy on £2,000 a week before bonuses complaining about travelling in for training. It got worse by the day. He hated the drive from his home in Oxford; he hated being away from his girlfriend; hated everything about being at West Ham. The other players had no time for him. We couldn't get him to raise a gallop in training and when we went to Scotland on a pre-season tour he was on the phone to his girlfriend for hours on end every day. It was pathetic, so pitiful that I almost felt sorry for him. We played a friendly at Southend before the season started and he was given a torrid time by West Ham fans who chanted 'Mummy's boy' and 'What a waste of money' at him all night. He even claimed he'd received death threats from supporters. I'm not sure about the threats but he brought all the abuse on himself.

From day one he did nothing but sulk. He wouldn't talk to me or Billy, or even any of the other players. He said he wanted to carry on living in Oxford and we agreed to that, but he rang in one Friday to say he wouldn't be turning up because he was tired and stressed from sitting in a traffic jam. He drove Billy crazy. Bill had set such high standards as a player and he got fed up when other people didn't reach them. Was Beauchamp the straw that broke the camel's back for Bill? That's impossible to say, but when he quit he told me: 'I don't have to worry about things now, that this one doesn't want to come here or that one wants more money.'

Beauchamp's demands were unbelievable. He wanted £30,000 as a signing-on fee before he even kicked a ball for the club. Then he demanded £350,000 to leave the club. When I took over from Bill I made it my first task to get shot of Beauchamp. When he left the club it was like a black cloud had been lifted. But even though he'd apparently made this terrible mistake in joining us, it took him forever to agree a move to Swindon. Swindon gave us £200,000 and defender Adrian Whitbread, who was valued at around £500,000. That put us only slightly down because we'd made only an initial payment of £850,000 to Oxford. But even the manner of his move to Swindon left a bitter taste. He spoke with Swindon manager John Gorman, now Glenn Hoddle's right-hand man with England, and made more unbelievable demands which at one stage threatened to block the deal. By this stage relations between West Ham and Beauchamp were so strained that the PFA were representing the player. I thought that was out of order. Here they were demanding that we pay Beauchamp's signing-on fee when he hadn't tried a leg for us from day one.

A few days later Swindon rang me and said that they were unhappy with the way the deal was dragging on – unless it was finalized within a couple of hours, they were pulling out. I rang John Gorman's number at the club and the voice at the other end of the line was Beauchamp's. Unmistakeable.

'What the f*** is going on?' I shouted down the phone.

'Well they won't give me this and they won't give me that,' he began.

'You what?' I screamed. 'Don't you dare come back here. I never want to see your ugly mug again. You've been nothing but aggravation since you got here. You take what they're offering and stop being such a greedy bastard.'

Soon afterwards John phoned and told me Beauchamp had changed his mind and was signing for them after all. John knew about all the problems we'd had with the player, but like most managers he thought he could get the best out of him. In the event Beauchamp did nothing for Swindon but eventually went back to Oxford and looked like a world-beater. The boy can play, he's got great ability, it's just a pity that while at West Ham his attitude left much to be desired.

One of my most heated, but ultimately most satisfying bust-ups, was with Barry Fry, over an out of contract player. I was manager of Bournemouth at the time and I coveted above all a non-League player for Maidstone called Mark Newson, who played for the non-League international side. Barry, the then Maidstone manager, was asking for £70,000 for a player I rated very highly. About this time Newson had been invited by Spurs for a two-week trial at White Hart Lane and I heard on the grapevine that he'd been very impressive in a reserve match. I was considering making a bid for Mark when I got a phone call from someone at Maidstone. I can't reveal even now who that person was because he swore me to secrecy, but he's no longer at the club.

'Harry,' he said, 'I thought I'd mark your card about Mark Newson. He's not on a contract.'

This was staggering news because if true it meant I could get Newson on a free.

'He's never been registered as a Maidstone player,' I was assured. 'His contract is still in the drawer. He's a free.'

I couldn't believe it. How could Maidstone be so silly? I checked with the FA who confirmed that Newson was indeed a non-contract player. In other words if I offered him enough wages to tempt him to leave Maidstone, Bournemouth could get a player of his undoubted ability for nothing. I wasn't going to let this one slip by. Somehow I managed to track down Newson's home number and asked him to see me at Dean Court. He told me that although he thought he'd done well during his trial at Spurs, it looked as though nothing would come of it. I seized on this to sign him the following day, for nothing. What a coup!

I rang Barry Fry to tell him my good news. 'Hello Barry, Harry. Just thought I'd let you know we've signed Mark Newson.'

'What? You mean you want to sign Mark?' Barry said.

'No,' I said, 'I've just signed him.'

'What do you mean you've signed him? We haven't agreed a fee.'

'There is no fee,' I said.

'What are you on about?' He said. 'You're mad.'

'He's not registered,' I said, and waited for the explosion.

'Don't you f****** start that game with me. I'm telling you now, if you think you can do that to me there'll be two fellers coming to see you to shoot your f****** kneecaps off.'

'Unlucky Barry,' I said. 'You've come unstuck' and put the phone down.

Five minutes later the phone goes and it's the Maidstone chairman. 'Now look Harry, let's be sensible about this. We'll come and see you and we'll sort this out like gentlemen. You're right, we've made a mistake, Newson isn't registered, but let's play this fair, let's sort out a fee.'

I stuck to my guns, and told them that as Newson was a non-contract player there would be no fee and that as far as I was concerned he was already a Bournemouth player. Suddenly the chairman from being as nice as pie, trying to smooth me over, turned ugly. 'You're finished, son,' he told me just before I hung up.

Two minutes later the phone went again. It was Barry.

'There's two f****** geezers coming to see you. I'm telling you now there's two f****** geezers coming and you're f****** dead. You won't have any kneecaps, Redknapp.'

'Unlucky Barry,' I said laughing, and put the phone down again.

Barry, his chairman and secretary came to see me two days later after things had calmed down, no doubt thinking I'd be prepared to offer some cash but they hit a brick wall. I wouldn't budge, not an inch, and they stormed out. Mark signed for us, was quickly made captain, and for five years was superb for us until I sold him to Fulham for £100,000.

Things never really got out of hand with Barry, despite his threats, but David Mellor is someone I'd happily take a swing at. Why the hell do football fans bother ringing his radio show? What does he know about football? If it was someone like Alan Hansen, fair enough, he'll have a valid opinion, but where is Mellor's football background? He's the classic example of an MP, or rather a failed MP, jumping on the football bandwagon to boost his own image. I heard him on the radio during the World Cup criticizing Glenn Hoddle's tactics. How is David Mellor qualified to give Glenn advice on managing an international side? The man's a fool and I've got no time for him at all.

There is, as you've probably guessed, a personal side to all this. It was my turn during 1997 to be picked on by the all-knowing Mellor. He took a pop at anything I did in the transfer market, in particular urging Pierre Van Hooijdonk not to join West Ham from Forest because we were bound to go down. He took an easy swipe at my signings of Florin Raducioiu and Marco Boogers, and he really put the boot in when I swooped for John Hartson and Paul Kitson. How could I pay £5 million for an Arsenal reserve, he asked. Well he even got the fee wrong. It was only £3 million, and John's worth considerably more than that now. I don't mind criticism but it's nice to know that the people who are sticking the knives in know exactly what they are talking about. Just look at Mellor. Can you imagine him ever playing football at school? Not everyone can play professional football but you've got to have some background, some natural love of the game. There was a time when I was so sick of his voice that I simply turned off the radio. I'm astonished his programme attracted so many listeners – it couldn't have been anything to do with the quality of his arguments.

My first year as manager of West Ham, difficult enough as I've already explained, was made harder still by the presence of a spy in the camp. When I first took charge at the club in August 1994 there was a little group of players at the club who couldn't behave themselves. They were forever having booze-ups and causing aggravation. Dale Gordon was the head of the club's entertainment committee and for the Christmas do he wanted to hire an open-top bus to trawl through London's West End.

'Are you out of your mind?' I said to him. 'We're struggling in the League and you want to go to the West End in an open-top bus like you've just won the bleedin' FA Cup. What the bloody hell are you thinking of?' So instead they hired a mini-bus to take them to the Apollo Restaurant in Stratford. One or two of them had too much to drink and set light to the seats on the bus at the end of the night. The big Dutch lad Jeroen Boere could be a handful after a few drinks and someone said he may have been involved. That's a symptom of how things were at the club at the time. We got a letter from the bus company demanding payment for repairs and so on, and I put it for safe keeping in the drawer of my desk at our Chadwell Heath training ground. In a separate incident three months later the same group of lads caused damage in the room of the Dormy Hotel near Bournemouth after a friendly at Dorchester. Again we received a letter of complaint from the hotel manager, and again I put the letter for safe keeping in my office.

A few weeks later all hell let loose. Someone had pilfered the letters from my draw and sent copies to the *Daily Mirror*. I woke up one morning to find both incidents were back page news.

'West Ham players wrecked two coaches and trashed a hotel room, the *Daily Mirror* can reveal today. Hammers stars, it is alleged, threw booze on carpets, food on walls, and smashed glasses in room 164 of the Dormy Hotel, near Bournemouth, after a friendly at Dorchester. In an internal memo sent to the hotel's general manager Derek Silk, there was an incredible list of the damage caused in the first-floor room. The room took two days to clean and the memo revealed there was:

- Alcohol spilled over the carpet in the bedroom
- Alcohol spilled over one of the single mattresses in the bedroom
- Glass smashed over the carpet
- Food scattered over the walls and carpets, behind beds and in beds
- Three pint glasses broken
- Bedspreads covered in food and alcohol

The bill for cleaning, replacements, labour and room out of

service for two days was £270. A snooker-table baize cover in the hotel club room was ripped, costing £210. The hotel sent Hammers manager Harry Redknapp – who wasn't involved – a letter explaining: "There is an extra invoice for £531.63 apart from the normal accommodation and extra charges."

'And in another separate incident two coaches were damaged when players were on their way to a party at the Apollo Restaurant in Stratford. A coach was ruined and more damage was caused to the replacement. Documents the *Mirror* has seen reveal in detail that:

'Seats in the first vehicle were urinated on. One was slashed needing re-upholstering and the coach had to be valeted with the loss of one day's hire. The bill was £500.

'A second coach's rear emergency window was broken, an interior light was smashed, seats were urinated on and a full valet was needed, again with one day's hire lost. The bill came to £662.'

Clearly this didn't put me in the best of moods, not because of the high jinks of the players – I'm not excusing their behaviour for a minute, it was clearly unacceptable and the people concerned are no longer at the club – but because a sneak had obviously stolen the letters from my desk to be photocopied. I said at the time that I was going to do everything in my power to nail the mole. You've got to be sick in the head to do something like that, I said, and everyone at the club was disgusted by it. I suspected at the time who the mole was, and my suspicions were later confirmed.

In a revamp of my backroom staff I'd let go a feller who I think resented me. He felt he should have been offered a job on the coaching staff. As an act of revenge, he took the letters from my desk and sent copies to the *Mirror*. But he reckoned without the investigative powers of Inspector Redknapp of the Yard. From a friend at the *Mirror* I got the envelope the mole had mailed to the newspaper and took it to a handwriting expert, along with an example of his writing. It was confirmed to my satisfaction that the writing was the same and the person was rumbled. It was sad that anyone should be so vindictive but I suppose that's life.

Many fans will recall the well-publicized bust-up I had on the pitch with Tottenham's Colin Calderwood at White Hart Lane, in January 1998. Just before half-time, Samassi Abou had a little kick at Ramon Vega, who went down like he was dead, a trend we saw so often and so maddeningly during France '98. The linesman attracted the attention of referee David Elleray, who I suppose had no alternative but to send Abou off. Abou thought he was hard done by and was arguing heatedly, apparently refusing to walk, and Elleray asked for my assistance to get Abou off the pitch before the situation got even more out of hand. I walked on to the pitch and as I did so, Calderwood came storming over. 'What the f***'s it got to do with you?' he shouted.

'I'm trying to get Abou off,' I said.

'Get the f*** off the pitch. It's nothing to do with you,' he said, and pushed me towards the touchline. I'm afraid I couldn't stand for that and pushed him back. Next minute John Hartson came rushing in from nowhere and bundled Calderwood out of the way, and I think Colin thought it was wiser to keep quiet. That's typical of John. I've got a great relationship with him and I think he thought he was my minder. If I was a player now, I think John and I would be great mates. I've always got on well with Colin Calderwood too, right from my Bournemouth days, and it was all forgotten afterwards. But the incident did bring into the spotlight the problem of players trying to get opponents booked and sent off. Vega only got up when he noticed Abou had got a red card, and I thought that was bad. Managers can only do so much to nip this trend in the bud. Perhaps it's time the players' union, the PFA, issued instructions to players that such behaviour will not be tolerated. In the long run it will drive fans away.

I have had my share of scrapes during my career, but having bust-ups are part of football, part of management. You name me a Premiership boss who hasn't at some stage fallen out big time with colleagues or former colleagues. It's part of the job, a job I still love and always will.

CHAPTER 13

Jamie and Louise

I'm the father-in-law of the girl voted the sexiest on the planet and that will be the cue in most pubs up and down the land for ribald comments of the nudge-nudge wink-wink variety. But songstress Louise, who married Jamie in Bermuda in July 1998, is the most down-to-earth girl you could hope to meet. She may be a pop-star temptress to the youngsters who read those laddish magazines but to me she's just a lovely girl who's married to my youngest son.

Louise, who made it big with chart-toppers Eternal before becoming a major pop star in her own right, is the least showbizzy person you could imagine. She's so shy and quiet away from the spotlight that I can't believe she has the front to go live on stage in front of thousands of people. I see her in those glamorous videos for her latest record and find it impossible to reconcile the sexy image I see on screen with the Louise who comes round to my home with Jamie for Sunday dinner. Jamie and her make a lovely couple, so Sandra and I were thrilled when the two of them got married. Jamie couldn't have met a nicer girl. She's a very caring person.

To give you an example of how unpretentious she is, I remember an occasion in 1997 when she did a concert in Leicester. She was due to travel to Bournemouth later that night because Jamie was back home with Sandra and I. But she rang to say she was going to be late because first the backing group needed to be dropped off in London before she could be driven to Bournemouth. She didn't reach us until 3am the following morning. I would have thought that someone of her stature was entitled to demand to be taken care of first. But Louise is not like that. She's not at all pushy. I think I'm a good judge of character, Sandra too, and we recognize her as one of us. There's no side to her, nothing big time about her at all. She's just a lovely girl.

Jamie and Louise decided to get married in Bermuda because they wanted to avoid all the publicity such a wedding was bound to generate in Britain. I don't think Jamie wanted another Gazza-type wedding, so it was mostly just the family there, with Mark the best man. Jamie's Liverpool team-mate Phil Babb was the only footballer there. The one disappointment was that my mum and dad weren't there to see their grandson get married, but neither of them will fly.

Jamie and Louise initially turned down a small fortune from *Hello!* magazine for a wedding photo spread until Louise was persuaded by her forceful manager that it would be good publicity. *Hello!* offered an incredible £300,000 and I couldn't believe it when Jamie at first turned that kind of dough down. But a couple of days before the *Hello!* issue was out on the streets, snatched pictures of the wedding, real poor-quality stuff, appeared in the rival *OK* magazine and *Hello!* got the hump. They came back and said that as the pictures were no longer exclusive their cash offer had to be reduced to £70,000. I think Jamie told them to bugger off – he'd never been interested in the first place.

I'm often asked what I think of Louise as a singer and I honestly do think she's great. That's not just proud father-in-law-speak. I thought Eternal were great, and I still think that about Louise now that she's a solo artist. She's a genuine singer with a great voice. She's not like these pop groups you get nowadays where they get four or five people together because they fit a certain image, not because they can sing. She met Jamie a few years ago when Jamie and some of his Liverpool team-mates went to watch a Take That concert. Eternal were on the bill too, and Jamie met Louise backstage. They went out a few times on and off after that, but I think it took a while before they became serious.

While it's fair to say that Jamie, by virtue of being a key player in the Liverpool team, and Louise, because she's a chart-topping singer, are a high-profile couple, they don't go out of their way to court publicity, and I think in a way that's protected Jamie from the sort of abuse Manchester United's David Beckham receives from football fans. Don't get me wrong, Jamie takes his fair share of stick on the field, but that's because of what he does or doesn't do as a footballer, not because of who he is married, or was engaged, to. Beckham on the other hand was taunted unmercifully by fans, even before the events in France '98, because of his relationship with one of the Spice Girls.

I think David wants to be more high-profile. He revels in it, his Spice Girl too, and that's possibly their problem. Jamie, Louise and Sandra bumped into Posh Spice, aka Victoria Adams, while Christmas shopping in London in 1997. Victoria had arrived in a big stretch limo, whereas Louise was wearing a baseball cap and trainers. The two singers began chatting about their Christmas Day plans. Louise said she was cooking Christmas dinner for her and Jamie, her very first attempt at it, while Posh Spice was having private caterers in, £200 a head, all that nonsense. They're different, aren't they? Nothing wrong with that of course, but I don't think you'd catch Jamie wearing a skirt like Beckham so famously did. He and Louise just want to be like any other normal couple.

Jamie's a good lad, popular wherever he goes. He has a cleaner who tidies his flat in Liverpool and he loves her, a real old Liverpool girl. She was speaking to Michael Owen, who was giving her a lift home from Jamie's one day, and told him what a nice lad she thought Jamie was. Michael told her that if he was half as well liked at Liverpool as Jamie, he'd be well pleased. That's the kind of feller Jamie is. Everyone loves him. It's the same with all the England lads. Wrighty idolizes him. Gazza, Incey, Macca – they're on the phone to him every minute. He's just one of those lads, gets on well with everybody.

I know Jamie's known as one of the pin-ups of the football world but he hates all that, it really embarrasses him. He got some stick at Liverpool when he did a bit of modelling a few years ago and now he doesn't want to know about it. He could make a fortune from it and in my view he should take full advantage. Other players are copping dough from it, why not him? He's turned down offers galore because all he wants to do is play football. At the end of the day no one gives a monkey's about you once your career's over so in my view you should make the bucks while you can. One of my most saddening sights was seeing Bobby Moore sitting in the back of the stands at Grimsby, eating fish and chips out of a newspaper and freezing his nuts off, just to earn a couple of bob helping out a radio station. This was the England captain who lifted the World Cup but no one gave a shit. I've always said to Jamie: 'Do your best, don't rip anybody off on the way, but if there's a chance to earn a few quid, take it because it doesn't last forever.'

Though Jamie's career in modelling was only brief, he and a few of his Liverpool team-mates have been saddled with this Spice Boys image and it really gets up his nose and mine. I know how dedicated to football Jamie, and the likes of Robbie Fowler and Steve McManaman, are. Jamie's always on the training ground, even long after training has finished. I don't know how they got stuck with this Spice Boys tag. Maybe it was because of an article based on comments Stan Collymore made after he quit Anfield. If it was, then that's absurd because Stan is the last person to criticize anyone else's dedication to football.

I was as gutted as Jamie when he had to pull out of the England World Cup squad for France '98 through injury. He's had two years of injuries and I believe it really has held him back. The ironic thing is, until the last two years I've never known Jamie to have an injury. From the time he was eight or nine I can't remember him missing a single game. I'm convinced that he played for months on a broken ankle. He first sustained the injury against Scotland during Euro '96, and every time he made a comeback for Liverpool the following season he'd be in agony for days after each game. He kept going but he knew deep down it wasn't right. Then at the end of that season he played for England in a friendly against South Africa and got an innocuous tap on the ankle. It was a mild challenge, not enough to inflict damage, but Jamie was in agony and the specialist, after diagnosing a fractured ankle, said the fracture was long-standing. In the 1997–98 campaign he finally looked to be free of problems and was playing really well leading up to the end of the season when he damaged his knee ligaments after a challenge by Coventry's Dion Dublin. But for that injury he was a certainty to be in the World Cup squad. If Glenn Hoddle had wanted to leave him out, the injury was the perfect excuse, but Glenn gave Jamie right up to the last minute to prove his fitness.

I speak to Jamie most days on the phone, and I'll always watch him if Liverpool are playing on a Sunday. Sandra and I have a meal with Jamie after an Anfield game, maybe a Chinese somewhere, and we drive home afterwards. Jamie gets home to Bournemouth when he can.

I must admit Jamie has recommended one or two players to me in the past, but he hasn't got the best of records. His last one was Don Hutchison, whose talent is not in doubt but who will be the first to admit he was disappointing in the short time he was at West Ham. He got into bad company, and I'm talking about at Upton Park. The crowd I had at West Ham at the time could be a handful and Don was easily led. They were a bad influence on him and he went off the rails a bit. He was moody, he had days when he didn't want to train, and he wouldn't put it all in. If he was at West Ham now I'm sure he'd be a totally different proposition because the players I have now all work hard, and are responsible professionals.

The games I look forward to the least every season are, because of Jamie, against Liverpool. It's the Liverpool result I look for first on a Saturday after our match, and I always dearly love to see them win. A few years ago we met Liverpool in the penultimate game of the season desperately needing to win to avoid relegation. Jamie was playing for the Reds, who were out of the title race and had nothing to play for. We won 3–0 and I can understand why sceptics beforehand might have thought that Jamie would take his foot off the gas. But there was no way he could afford to do that because he knew people would be watching him. There was no way he wanted to do that because he's a professional footballer and professional footballers as a breed want to win, no matter if it's the World Cup Final or an eight-a-side match in training.

Two of the proudest moments in my life were when Jamie made his Liverpool debut and again when he made his full England debut. It was fantastic to see him progress to that level after watching him kick a ball around from when he was a toddler. In fact he's been football mad since he was old enough to walk. When he was about 10 he got kicked out of the district team because they were worried he was playing too much football, and for his Sunday team he was the first to turn up every week. But how could he not be a footballer? From the age of four or five he was on the training ground all day with me while I was playing in America. All he did for hours on end was kick a ball around, rubbing shoulders with the likes of Bobby Moore, Geoff Hurst, and Alan Hudson. And back in Bournemouth – Sandra will kill me when she reads this – when I was supposed to drop him off at school I'd take him instead to training with me, taking him home at 4pm and pretending he'd spent the day at school. God knows what the teachers thought, but I think Sandra became a little suspicious when she found out he couldn't read or write! I always knew Jamie was going to be a footballer, so I thought his time would be better spent learning his trade.

He was at Tottenham when he was 11 and Peter Shreeves used to let him from time to time train with the first team – that's how advanced he was. He even took him on a first-team trip to Southampton when he was 12. Someone once reported Jamie for not being the right age when he was playing in the Bournemouth Under-11 League. They were right – he was only seven. He's always loved being involved with players much older than himself.

Jamie made his professional debut for Bournemouth as a 16-year-old at, believe it or not, West Ham. It was in April 1990, the year we got relegated from the Second Division – there was no Premiership at that time, remember – and I had to call on Jamie because of a terrible injury crisis. To be honest we'd done ever so well being in that division in the first place. It was one of my greatest achievements as a manager when we went up as Third Division champions in 1986–87 when I won the manager of the year award. My star midfielder Shaun Brooks fell ill on the coach on the way to the game and the only possible replacement was Jamie. Paul Miller, my skipper and the only experienced outfield player I could call on, urged me to pick Jamie. It was against my better judgement but I had no choice. We got beat 4–1, no surprise, but Jamie played really well, never giving the ball away once against a useful Hammers side still bidding for promotion to the top flight.

Soon afterwards I went to a dance in London in honour of Brian Clough. Sandra and I were on the floor at the end of the night when we bumped into Kenny Dalglish and his wife Marina. Kenny was Liverpool boss of course at the time. We got chatting and he said he'd heard my young lad was a useful player.

'Can I have a look at him at Anfield for a week?' he asked.

To be honest I wasn't really that keen. Jamie had been at Bournemouth for only about six months and I thought it better for him to stick around for a couple of years or so. But Jamie was really keen to give it a try. On the Monday, his first day at Liverpool, I got a call from Dean Court while I was in the car.

'Harry, where are you? Kenny Dalglish has rang six times.'

'Oh no,' I thought. 'Something must have happened to Jamie. He must have broken his leg or something.'

I punched Kenny's office number on the mobile and he answered.

'Kenny. Harry here. What's up?' I asked nervously.

'Hello Harry,' he said calmly. 'Any more like Jamie at home?'

To say he was impressed with Jamie was an understatement. He said he wanted to sign him there and then and when I suggested he should take a look at him for the week he practically barked at me that he didn't have to, that he'd already seen enough. But Jamie was worried. He didn't think he'd ever get into the Liverpool team and was looking to stay at Bournemouth for a bit longer. Kenny began ringing me every day, even Christmas day, to ask about Jamie, to ask whether we could do a deal. Eventually Jamie and I went to watch Liverpool play Blackburn in a cup replay and went for a Chinese meal with Kenny and Marina afterwards.

'Look', said Kenny. 'I want him. Whatever happens, Jamie's got to sign.'

Jamie was there but he was looking doubtful. 'I ain't gonna get in the Liverpool team, am I?' he said to Kenny.

Now I'm not doing the silly proud father bit here, but Kenny honestly told Jamie that not only would he get in the side, but that he was going to build a team around him.

So Jamie signed in January 1991 for a manager who clearly thought the world of him. A few weeks later Liverpool played Everton in that dramatic FA Cup fifth-round replay that finished 4–4 and a day later Kenny quit the club. Poor Jamie didn't know what had hit him. He idolized Kenny, had all his pictures on the wall, and now he'd gone and left. His whole life was upside down. I was choked. I wasn't bitter with Kenny, he obviously had his reasons for quitting, but I was very worried for Jamie. Graeme Souness took over and Jamie moaned to me that he'd been there three months and Souness had not said a word to him. 'He doesn't even know my name', he complained. He was in digs on his own right near Anfield and I could tell he was thinking of packing up. Come on, he was a 17-year-old lad on his own in a strange city. But all credit to him, he stuck it out and I remember him ringing me one day struggling to contain his excitement. It was the day of Liverpool's UEFA Cup tie in France against Auxerre, and Jamie said: 'I think I'm playing. I think I'm playing.' He did play, very well too, even though Liverpool lost. He loved Graeme after that and Graeme really took to him, too. When I was a teenager I always fancied myself as a player but Jamie is far better than I ever was. Different class in fact. The boy can play.

Mark, my eldest son, is a good player too and would definitely have made a living from the game if it wasn't for injury. He was a big defender who could really pass the ball superbly, but he broke his ankle very badly when he was 17 and that wrecked his chances. Even now he can hardly walk for a couple of days after a game. Mark's a football agent now, working for the sports wing of the Bank of Luxembourg, and I think he'll do really well. Mark and Jamie look very much alike and often get mistaken for each other. There have been one or two occasions when England managers have been told Jamie was seen knocking back lagers on the town when in fact he was tucked up in bed at the England HQ!

Jamie isn't the only professional footballer in the family of course. His cousin, my nephew, is young Frank Lampard. Frank's mother of course is Sandra's sister, Pat. I'm delighted Frank has become such a great player because there were one or two problems between Frank Snr and I when young Frank was just breaking into the first team. I was disappointed in certain sections of the West Ham crowd which gave him no end of stick during his early appearances. He was only an 18-year-old kid and his dad had been such a great player for the club that I found it hard to understand why they were so quick to dish out abuse. The crowd were getting at me for playing him, and Frank Snr felt I wasn't playing him enough. We never fell out over it, but I was aware that Frank thought I was bringing his son along too slowly. But I felt he was still maturing. I'd been through the same situation with Jamie and I was confident that what I was doing was correct.

So I was delighted to see young Frank prove everybody wrong with his fantastic performances during the 1997–98 season. He's going to be an outstanding player, destined for the very top. He's dedicated, he trains like a demon, he's a great lad, and he's got a great attitude. It will be a dream come true if he and Jamie, who are very close, play together in the same midfield for England. That would make two old-timers at West Ham very proud indeed.

CHAPTER 14

Trouble in Dicksy-land

When I first got to West Ham the club seemed to be built around Julian Dicks. He was a cult figure and no doubt an outstanding player but the influence he wielded was unhealthy. Dicksy didn't like running so pre-season training was an absolute nightmare. When we got the players on those marathon runs every club organizes before the start of a season, Dicksy didn't want to know. 'What's all this shit?' he would say. 'I'm not doing that crap.' Then his little acolytes would join forces with him and it was mayhem.

Dicksy's talent was not in doubt, but if I say he was a pest I am guilty of an outrageous understatement. He was, and I stress was, the most disruptive professional footballer I've ever come across. An absolute nightmare. The fans idolized him to an extent that was in many ways almost unacceptable. In one game at Derby he got sent off after 15 minutes for two yellow-card offences, two absolutely horrendous tackles. Yet for the next 75 minutes the visiting West Ham fans chanted his name.

That was completely out of order, because as far as I was concerned he'd let the team down. He'd made two diabolical challenges and deserved to be red-carded, leaving his 10 colleagues to work their socks off for an unlikely victory. Yet they didn't get a mention. It was all 'Julian Dicks this and Julian Dicks that.' That's how it was at West Ham at that time. It was all about Dicksy.

For someone with such immense talent, he was an appalling trainer. Every day he'd have a row with Bill over something petty. Bill would say it's a corner, Dicksy would argue it was a goal-kick. Then they'd have a blazing row and Dicksy would just walk off the training pitch. The feeling among the other players about Dicks was mixed. He had his little group of mates who loved him but if truth be known there was an equally large group glad to see the back of him once we off-loaded him to Liverpool. He was a very strong influence. A hard nut who had players happy to go along with him. Those who didn't get on with him didn't want to fall out with him.

Dicksy was no shrinking violet when it came to the physicals. After he had his first knee operation he had to wear a brace in his first game back. It was in a youth game over at our training ground at Chadwell Heath and the theory was that Dicksy would take things easy to test out the strength of his knee, which had been virtually rebuilt. That was the theory, but someone forgot to tell Dicksy. Within seconds of the kick-off the ball reached the opposition outside right. Before he even had a chance to get control of it Dicksy hit him with a tackle that had X-certificate stamped all over it. It was bonecrunching and almost sent the winger into orbit. But Dicksy was fine.

It was amazing, given the ferocity of his tackles and his near-obsessive hatred of training, that he wasn't always injured. In fact I don't think I ever saw him do a stretching exercise, and he couldn't touch his toes if you gave him 10 grand. During training, he'd be strolling around at the back as everyone was exercising, muttering to himself: 'What a load of bollocks.' But then once the ball came out he was like a man possessed. If the ball was there, he'd want to play for his life. With a ball, no one at the club had the quality Dicksy had. He could put it anywhere he wanted. His left foot was like a magic wand and he was the best header of the ball at the club, too. But he just wouldn't run. The only way we could get him to move was by putting the cones out and getting him to dribble the ball up and back around them. We had to invent all sorts of silly drills with the ball just to make him run.

But that said, he was a massive cult figure at Upton Park. This was mainly because of his fantastic ability but also partly because of his well-documented psycho tendencies. He could have played for England if his attitude and temperament had been better, but his attitude towards the national team was indifference. I think he went away with the England squad once but had a bust-up with someone which was absolutely no surprise. He'd have a row in an empty room! He just couldn't help himself.

I remember vividly my first day of pre-season training when I first joined West Ham in 1992. All the lads were there apart from you know who.

'Where's Dicksy?' I asked. 'He's the captain, isn't he?'

'Yeah,' someone said, 'but he hasn't got back from holiday yet.'

He'd had all the summer, yet he decided to come back a day late. Everyone else was there on time. He was a professional footballer, on big money, and had just had seven weeks off, yet to him it just didn't matter that he was a day late. That's how he was. That's how the club was. We had him in the office the next day and asked him to explain, but he couldn't understand what all the fuss was about. What difference does one day make, he said, shrugging his shoulders.

A few games into our first season back in the Premiership and we hadn't won a match – hadn't even looked like winning – and we were due to play at Coventry. The week before I decided to go up to watch a Liverpool game on a Sunday – they never seemed to be off telly in those days so loads of their games were on Sundays. Up at Anfield I got chatting to their manager Graeme Souness. Graeme asked me how things were going and I told him the truth. Badly. We hadn't even got anyone to sell, I told him. We were going to have to sell our best player.

'Who's that?' he asked.

'Julian Dicks,' I said. 'He's different class.'

Graeme's ears pricked up. 'He's that good, is he?'

I told him that he was, and that he'd kick lumps out of him (Graeme), even in training, and that's just what he wanted to hear. I think he loved the thought of the challenge. A kind of 'yeah, will he? I'll soon sort him out.' I think at the time Graeme wanted to switch things around a bit at Anfield, shake a few players up. So he told me that he'd come and give Dicksy the once-over at Coventry the following Saturday, with Liverpool again playing on the Sunday. We were 1–0 up on the day, playing brilliantly and looking like we were going to get our first win of the season, in front of the watching Souness. Then, just before half-time one of the Coventry players was wrestling with Dicksy for the ball and tugged Dicksy's shirt. Now Dicksy had only one response for such a situation, be it in training, five-a-side, or a full-scale match. He'd swing back his elbow and crack the opposing player in the face. That was always his first reaction. Crash.

Anyway, the Coventry player went down like a sack of spuds. 'Oh no,' I thought. 'We're down to 10 men again.' The crowd went barmy, but neither the referee nor the linesman had seen it. The ref stopped the game and consulted the linesman but by this stage I was beginning to think we had got a result. Sure enough, the ref only booked Dicksy because he was aware that something had gone on, but he didn't know exactly what. But it was a blatant sending-off. Everyone in the crowd saw it. The players came in at half-time and Bill had a right go at Dicksy.

'What are you doing? We're 1–0 up.'

'Ah piss off,' he told Bill, and next minute wanted to fight him in the dressing room. Then he threw a sulk, took his boots off, and refused to go out for the second half. It all got sorted out, he went out and played, and we ended up drawing 1–1, but I shuddered to think what Graeme Souness was thinking by this stage about his potential new signing.

But incredibly he was impressed. 'Did all right, Dicksy,' he said. 'Puts it about a bit, doesn't he?'

A couple of weeks later we were playing Swindon at home and Souness was there again. Dicksy's performance was okay, nothing great, but enough to convince the Anfield boss. 'Yeah, I'll have him,' he said.

The following Monday morning I was out training with the lads when the phone rang.

'Harry,' someone shouted. 'It's Graeme Souness.'

I picked up the receiver. 'Hello Graeme.'

No niceties, straight into business. 'I'll do a straight swap. You give us Dicksy, we'll give you David Burrows.'

'Leave it out, Graeme,' I told him. 'I can't do that. He's our best player.'

This went on, like two kids swapping their precious football cards. In the end, we got Burrows, a tough-tackling full-back, Mike Marsh, a clever midfielder, and £200,000. The money was very important. We hadn't got a striker who could score goals. Clive Allen was out injured, and we were desperate for a scorer. I knew Lee Chapman was available and I believed he could do a job for us, with £200,000 enough to sign him. So the deal was completed early that week. In September 1993, Bugsy Burrows, Marshy and Chapman joined us, and Dicksy went to Anfield.

I knew I'd be in for some stick from the fans. There was no doubt about it. As far as they were concerned they'd lost their best player – their cult hero. But they didn't know what had gone on behind the scenes. Our next game was at Blackburn and they didn't come much tougher than that. A strong contingent of fans travelled up to Ewood Park and I just knew that they were going to make their feelings known about the Dicks transfer. We had managed to scramble a 0–0 draw at Swindon the week before and though results were beginning to go our way it would only take defeat at Blackburn – a dead cert according to the bookmakers' odds that morning – for our fans in their current mood to turn against us. But we won 2–0, a fantastic result, and they were delighted. All of a sudden it was like, 'Oh well, Dicksy's gone, but we've got three new players.'

And looking back that was the turning point. We only lost twice (at Newcastle and Liverpool) in our next 10 games and suddenly the Dicks move was looking a great bit of business. Burrows was doing well, Marsh too, and though the crowd didn't take to Chapman I thought he did a good job for us.

Given all that had gone before it must have been a massive surprise to West Ham and all our supporters when I brought Dicksy back to the club, in October 1994. To be honest, even the dinner lady didn't want to see him again. But I think his experience at Liverpool humbled him. In his first spell at West Ham he was nothing but aggravation, but since his return he's been no trouble at all. Remember that we got a total of £2.5 million for Dicksy from Liverpool when you consider the value of the players we got in exchange, and that was a very good deal for the club. Souness wanted Dicks badly but in all honesty he was a disaster at Anfield. The crowd didn't take to him there like they did at Upton Park, and he let himself go a bit. I'm told that when he got to Liverpool he caused a stir the night before his very first game. It was an away match and an official came round asking all the players what they wanted for lunch the following day. Dicksy wanted fillet steak.

'No, we don't have fillet steak at Liverpool. You can have chicken, rice…'

Dicksy cut in. 'I want fillet steak,' he said. 'Medium rare.'

No, he was told, that wasn't an option.

'I want fillet steak, medium rare,' he repeated.

The next day he got fillet steak, medium rare, but I don't think he'd done himself any favours. He could pull that sort of stunt at West Ham where he was a big fish, but Liverpool were sure to sort him out. As it turned out I don't think they did. He was still overweight when he came back to us.

Liverpool were desperate to get rid of him. He was training with the kids and not even getting close to a first-team place. He was causing Liverpool the same problems as he'd caused us and they were looking to dump him, no matter how much they lost on the deal. So we were able to take him back on the cheap, just doing a deal on appearances. He had to play something like 200 games for us to pay £500,000. I thought at that money we couldn't lose.

All of a sudden Dicksy wasn't the big 'I am' when he returned to Upton Park. How could he be when he'd been such a failure at Liverpool? And he's been fantastic since his return, with a whole different outlook on life. Great on the pitch and no problem off it. He has even taken up golf and, hackneyed though it sounds, I honestly believe the game has changed him as a person. In golf there's no room for bad behaviour or bullying. He was even talking about taking up the game professionally if he doesn't recover fully from his current knee injury, but I think that idea will be put on hold following his magnificent comeback performance against Northampton in September 1998. He's had eight knee operations, has been told by everyone that his career was over, and then he goes and gives one of the greatest performances I've ever seen from a foot-baller. Dicksy had been a pest in the past but I have nothing but admiration for him now.

I've no doubt in my mind that within two or three years Rio Ferdinand will be the best defender in Europe, possibly even the world, but it took my old man Harry Snr to first alert me to what a talent we had in our midst. Looking at Rio now, in the

England World Cup squad while still a teenager, it's hard to believe that he was not one of the most sought-after young players as a schoolboy, but to be honest there was only ever West Ham and Millwall in the hunt for him. He was a good player, true, but as a 14-year-old he was not extra-special. In the few years he has been at Upton Park, however, he has improved beyond recognition, and it was after the final of the South East Counties League Cup Final, in May 1995, that we, or rather my dad, first realized what star quality we had on our hands.

We lost 5–2 to Chelsea at home in the first leg. Rio didn't play in that one but I was at the game and I must say we were slaughtered. The second leg at Chelsea was held the night before the first-team squad were due to fly off to Australia so I couldn't make it to the game, but I got a phone call from my dad immediately after the final whistle that night with news of a dramatic comeback. Chelsea had gone 1–0 up to make it 6–2 on aggregate, but the young Hammers had fought back brilliantly to win the leg 4–1 and take the final into penalties. Rio was among those to score from the spot, with young Frank Lampard clinching the deciding spot-kick. But it wasn't the spirited fightback that my dad wanted to talk about – he was breathless about the performance of a tall, slim lad in midfield who had run the whole show.

'What a player you've got there,' he said. 'I've never seen anyone like him,' he told me.

For the life of me I couldn't work out who he was talking about.

'You know,' he said. 'The big lad...' fumbling for the match programme, '...Ferdinand.'

'Oh yeah,' I said, thinking my dad had gone a bit nuts. I'd watched Rio in training for some time on Tuesday and Thursday nights and while we all thought he was okay, we'd seen little hint of the enormous talent that was to blossom.

'He was absolutely brilliant,' my dad went on. 'He was

picking the ball up in midfield and just floating past three or four players. Where the hell did you pick him up from?'

Sure enough, youth team coach Tony Carr repeated what my dad had said and we knew that Rio really was someone to keep a close eye on. He was only 15 then, still at school, but once he joined the club full time he went from strength to strength. You could almost notice the improvement on a daily basis.

Rio now is the most incredible player. He does not have a single fault. In training we regularly have one-against-one sessions and Eyal Berkovic, who has so many tricks up his sleeve that he can go past most people, moaned to me: 'That Rio, I just can't beat him. He is impossible.' And it's true. I have never seen a single player beat him one against one. He has so much pace that if someone knocks the ball past him he just moves up a gear. When Jamie was training with the England team shortly before having to pull out of the 1998 World Cup squad through injury, he phoned me full of admiration for Rio. 'Dad,' he said. 'That Rio. No one can get past him. He's unbelievable.'

Rio has everything. He's good in the air, strong, quick, and even though he's only 19 he's so composed on the ball. In his first full season one of his first matches was against Les Ferdinand and Spurs at Upton Park. Les can be a real handful for anyone, but Rio didn't give him a kick. I thought to myself that if he can do that to Les then he's definitely going places. We went to Newcastle soon afterwards and he did the same to Alan Shearer. It's frightening to think how good he can become.

I've always been keen on one-against-one sessions in training. It brings out the best in defenders and forwards and I think it's interesting to see who has the best technique. Stan Lazaridis regularly impresses in such sessions because of his lightning pace. He can push the ball past a player and do him for pace before getting a shot on target. He wouldn't beat Rio, but he would go past nine out of 10 defenders. Frank Lampard can also make a yard of space in such situations and regularly hits the target. John Hartson's not a dribbler but he can't half finish when he makes space, and Trevor Sinclair's got the pace and the skill to excel in one-on-ones.

Lazaridis has been a real find for us but he arrived at Upton Park from the unlikeliest of sources. We'd been invited during 1995 to a summer trip to Australia but as that season drew to a close I thought we'd be pulling out. It was my first season as manager, we were staring relegation full in the face and I thought there was no way I could stomach a trip to the other side of the world if all that awaited us on our return was life in Division One. A season earlier Sheffield United, then managed by my mate Dave Bassett, had planned a similar trip Down Under, only to fly out as a relegated club, and I thought the same was going to happen to us. But we managed to claw our way to safety and flew to Australia in a much brighter frame of mind than I ever thought possible. Because of prior engagements I missed our first game on the Australian tour but Frank filled me in during a phone call.

'It went well,' he said, 'but Timmy (Breacker) got a chasing off their left-winger.'

'Really?' I said. 'Who was that?'

'Don't know. Young geezer. Wasn't half quick.'

When I got to Australia I immediately made enquiries about this flying left-winger. I found out it was Stan, and that his club wanted £200,000 – the price clearly having risen once it became clear an English Premiership club was interested. We had him over at West Ham for a couple of weeks on a trial basis, and he impressed us again so we were only too happy to cough up the cash. Unfortunately, Stan broke his leg soon after arriving at the club and it took him a bit of time to settle, but he's got better and better and is now a very influential member of the team. Terry Venables thought the world of him when he was Australian team coach, and Arsene Wenger has told me a few times how highly he rates him, so for £200,000 he's proven a real bargain. Indeed Stan has been such a success for us that we have now set up a special soccer academy in Australia. We employ coaches over there and any talented youngsters that come through we would expect them to end up here. I have one or two reports in my drawer about promising youngsters Down Under, so watch this space.

If you think Australia is a strange breeding ground for a top-class Premiership player, then what about Israel, home of our midfield playmaker Eyal Berkovic? He had a terrific first season for us and I know that every goal he scores for us, every top-class performance he gives, rubs salt in the wounds of Spurs chairman Alan Sugar, who thought he was nailed on to sign Berkovic before we did. We'd agreed a fee with his club Maccabi Haifa – when he played for Southampton in his first season in the Premiership it was only on a loan basis – but then heard on the grapevine that Spurs were sniffing around. At first I thought it was just a ploy by Maccabi to jack up his fee, but Peter Storrie found out from Sugar that Spurs were genuinely in the hunt.

'Given a choice between Spurs and West Ham, Berkovic is bound to join us', said Sugar smugly, firmly believing Tottenham's huge Jewish following would influence the little Israeli's decision. Berkovic met with Spurs boss Gerry Francis before coming to see me. We agreed to match the terms Spurs had offered, and he opted to sign for West Ham instead of our London rivals. It was a big surprise, especially to me as I really did think Spurs held all the trump cards. But Berkovic liked the plans I had in mind for him, playing in a free role behind the front two, and possibly that swung it. After he had signed for us Sugar said he'd only ever wanted Berkovic as a squad player anyway. Sour grapes or what!

The bust-up between Eyal and John Moncur during the first half of our match at Chelsea in November 1997 shocked most fans but I must admit I could see it coming. John and Stevie Lomas had been getting on Eyal's case a bit because they thought that when he didn't have the ball he wasn't doing enough work. John gave him a rollicking during this Chelsea game and Eyal lost his head, pushing him in an incident that looked as if it could develop into a full-scale fight. The dressing room wasn't a happy place at half-time as both players were still clearly furious about what had gone on. It wasn't easy to sort it all out with both players still shouting and hollering, but to be fair to Eyal, John and Stevie had given him a hard time. Every time something went wrong they were jumping at him, and I could sense something was coming. We've all got our different strengths in football and Berkovic isn't going to run all day and throw himself into 50-50 tackles, but he can play passes no one else would even think about. I think John and Eyal have come to respect each other a lot more now – they each recognize their respective strengths and weaknesses – and though there was an uneasy atmosphere between them shortly after the Chelsea incident, everything's fine now.

Berkovic is a terrific footballer, one of the most talented I've ever worked with. When you look at him he looks more like a jockey than a top-class footballer, but he's a model professional. He trains hard, he's very punctual, and rarely misses a game through injury. John Moncur is a real character at West Ham, the club comic, and an absolute nutter. I remember one day when the rain was chucking it down at our Chadwell Heath training ground. I'd never seen rain like it, absolutely torrential, but when I glanced out of the window I saw the lone figure of John Moncur, completely starkers except for a pair of socks and football boots, diving into puddles. He's a very popular figure at the club, and a very talented footballer. He's no mean golfer either with a handicap of two.

We've got a great blend of youth and experience at the club now, especially following the signings in the summer of 1998 of Ian Wright and Neil Ruddock. The camaraderie is excellent. I wouldn't say the camaraderie was bad when I first arrived at the club, but then it was all about where the players were going drinking that night; now football is the main topic of conversation.

Wright and Ruddock are important to us, not just because of their obvious abilities but because of the presence they bring to a dressing room. While I was delighted with our efforts in finishing so high in the Premiership at the end of the 1997–98 campaign, I was a little disturbed how quiet the dressing room was. Rio Ferdinand and Frank Lampard will go on to be powerful figures in the camp, no doubt about that, but that season was their first full campaign and you can't expect players of their tender experience to be acting like Tony Adams on match days.

Every manager is looking for an Adams figure, for that ability to gee players up in the dressing room. Jamie told me that during Euro '96 he couldn't believe the influence Adams had on the rest of the camp. He made Terry Venables' job easy, Jamie told me. But there aren't many Tony Adamses around. I suppose Glenn Hoddle will be thankful for that. Despite what Glenn said, I'm sure he was hurt by the comments Adams made about him in his autobiography *Addicted*. Adams is perhaps at the stage of his career where he doesn't worry how many feathers he ruffles, but I would be bitterly disappointed if any of my players came out and made similar comments about me while I was still their manager. I'm sure it cannot do anything to improve relations in the dressing room.

To give you an example of the influence Wrighty and Ruddock have had at West Ham, just look at how the side bounced back to beat Liverpool after suffering a catastrophic loss at home to Wimbledon three days earlier at the start of the 1998–99 season. We were 3–0 up inside half an hour against Wimbledon and looking like running up a cricket score. But all of a sudden they pushed four 6ft-plus players up front, our new Chilean defender Javier Margas didn't know what had hit him, and we lost 4–3. I must admit I went into a depression for about two days after that one. I guess most football supporters expected me to storm into the dressing room after the final whistle and read the riot act to my players, but experience has taught me that very often such strong-arm tactics backfire. All you get in the next game is a team short of confidence, a team almost expecting to lose. So instead I told my players that such a 90 minutes could only ever happen against Wimbledon, a real one-off team, and that it would never happen again as long as they were in the Premiership.

I was anxious before the Liverpool game three days later to see what the mood in the dressing room would be. I'd have understood if the players were feeling nervous. After all they'd thrown away a 3–0 lead at home against a team rated by bookmakers as relegation contenders, and were facing another home game in front of the same fans just a few days later. But I needn't have worried. There was Ruddock playing Elvis Presley songs full blast in the dressing room, with Wrighty doing his best Elvis impression, collar turned up, that kind of thing. All the rest of the players were singing at the top of their voices. And this minutes before a match against the Premiership leaders at the time.

Ruddock has trained brilliantly since he's been at the club, his weight problems are a thing of the past, and he's brought a much-needed aggressive attitude to the side. Wrighty's outlook has been a breath of fresh air. Here's a player who's been there, done it, and bought the T-shirt, but he's still full of enthusiasm for everything he does and he's the perfect role model for youngsters at the club. I know John Hartson was overawed by Wrighty when they played together for a short time at Arsenal but now they make a superb partnership.

I've always loved Wrighty, on and off the field. He's a fantastic player and a fantastic goalscorer and I was delighted to clinch his signature in the summer of 1998. I realize he gives the impression with his off-the-field antics, like hosting a TV chat show or making a pop record, of not being entirely serious, but every time I've been in his company I've been struck by how dedicated he is to the game. He stays off the drink, eats the right food, does everything to make sure he gets the best out of his career and I've a lot of time for that outlook.

I think he'll be a great influence on Hartson, although I can understand why some Hammers fans worry a little about the poor disciplinary record of both players. John will be the first to admit that most of his bookings and sendings-off have been for silly things, punching somebody or giving someone a slap. He doesn't need to do that, he's a good enough player without bringing that sort of thing into his game. The only problem with John Hartson is that he doesn't realize how good he is, or how good he can become. I want him to be aggressive, but not to retaliate.

As I've said earlier in the book I have a lot of time for John. He's probably the only punter apart from myself at the club. He loves a bet, and will often on away trips act as the team bookie. If we're in a hotel on a Friday night he'll lay bets on the live Sky match that night. Same with the big golf tournaments. For the Open at Royal Birkdale in the summer of 1998, though, it was John Moncur who acted as bookie and he absolutely cleaned up when Mark O'Meara won the title. Not a single player had backed O'Meara.

Stevie Lomas, the captain, is a presence at West Ham, but he leads by example on the field more than exerting influence in the dressing room. Paul Kitson's a very quiet lad, and though Trevor Sinclair's bubbly, he's not one to be shouting or striving to get his point across at half time. Hartson may give the impression, perhaps because of his disciplinary record, of being an overpowering figure but even he is quiet on match days. There's nothing wrong with that, but every manager will tell you you've got to have leaders, you've got to have voices in the dressing room. There's nothing worse than silence among the players in the hour leading up to a game. Wrighty and Ruddock have that bit of bounce to gee players up when things aren't going right.

Trevor Sinclair was a big hit in his first season with us towards the end of the 1997–98 campaign but I was warned off buying him by Colin Todd, the Bolton manager. Toddy had seen Sinclair play a couple of days before our interest became known and he said to me: 'What do you want to buy him for? I saw him the other night and he was a disgrace. He's got a big fat arse.'

But I've known Trevor since he was a kid and I knew that his career had gone stale with QPR. As their fortunes plummeted, so too did Trevor's and he just needed a fresh start. That was why we got him for £1.6 million when a couple of years earlier he was valued at £7 million.

I've always said goalkeepers are a different breed and the three at West Ham certainly are. Ludo Miklosko, Shaka Hislop and Craig Forrest are all very good keepers, talented enough each to be first choices in Premiership sides. All are great trainers but all keep themselves to themselves. They are worked hard by our goalkeeping coach Les Sealey, who's a real character in his own right. Ludo is one of the best trainers I've ever seen. He's in his mid-30s now but he keeps himself so fit and I'm convinced he'll make a great goalkeeping coach when he quits playing. Ludo was brought up in Czechoslovakia and like most sportsmen from that part of Europe is 100 per cent dedicated to his trade. In my opinion he is one of the best goalkeepers in West Ham's history.

Of the long-standing Hammers players, you know Steve Potts and Tim Breacker will never let you down. They're real family lads, good pros who've seen hundreds of comings and goings over the years but have remained loyal to West Ham.

Ian Pearce was a big success for us when he joined us from Blackburn in 1997–98. People don't realize the pace Pearcey has – he's a real flying machine – but again he barely opens his mouth in the dressing room. I surprised a few people when I played Pearce at right-wing-back against Leeds during his first season with us but he did fantastically for me. In fact he could even do a good job for me up front. If he pushed himself a little more, believed in himself a little more, showed a little more determination, he could go all the way because he's got everything. I'm hoping that as his career develops he shows that little bit of extra drive that makes the difference between a good player and an outstanding player.

And while we're talking of outstanding players, I have a youngster who could develop into just that in a few years. Joe Cole is still only 16 but he has incredible potential. When I first saw him as a 14-year-old I couldn't believe what I was seeing. He could do everything. But I don't want to put too much pressure on the lad. The country is full of superstar teenagers who didn't make the grade as professionals. All I will say is that I've never seen a better prospect as a 14-year-old in all my years in football. If he continues to progress at his current rate, he will be a top-class player.

Most football fans have a certain image of Premiership players, that when they're not training or playing they're in nightclubs chatting up Page 3 models and generally living the fast life. Well I can't speak for the players of other clubs, but that's definitely not true of the West Ham lads. I've pretty much got a bunch of married lads here. They're mostly settled, which makes my job easier because I'm not worrying all the time about their whereabouts. I suppose Rio Ferdinand and Frank Lampard, being the youngest members of the side, get most of the attention from the girls who like to taste the glamour of Premiership football, but even those two recognize the sacrifices they have to make if they are to stay at the top of their profession. Players have to be careful because there's always a bird willing to earn a few bob by selling a story to a newspaper about a famous footballer's bedroom habits and prowess, giving him marks out of 10 or some other nonsense. That's how football's gone. Big business, yes, but that means there's always someone out there looking to make a few quid by telling a story about you. So the young players have to be very very careful about how they behave off the pitch.

About four years ago we were training at Chadwell Heath

one Saturday morning when suddenly there was a big punch-up between ex-Hammers Alvin Martin and Matthew Rush. Alvin, a long-established pro, reacted badly to a tackle from young Rushy and next second they were at each other's throats. Within half an hour I got a phone call from a national newspaper reporter wanting to know more about this big fight at West Ham's training ground. One of the fans who'd come to watch us training had raced off the moment the punch-up had finished and tipped off the paper to earn a few bob. That just shows you that little that happens at a football club, little that players do off the field, will remain secret for long and that's why they have to be ever so careful.

Top-class players in England nowadays earn crazy money, let's be honest about it, but then so too do their counterparts in golf, tennis, or a host of other sports. The Sky money has come into football, big sponsorship money too, and top players can earn fortunes. But not all. Lower-division players are still earning around £300 or £400 a week and there's an awful lot more of them than those earning £10,000 a week. Yet should we complain about such astronomical wages? Surely if that's what the market is prepared to pay, then we should just accept it. We can't expect players to say 'oh no, I can't accept £10,000 a week, it's far too much' if clubs are prepared to pay that sort of dough. The grounds are full and the clubs able to pay these sort of wages aren't losing money. We pay good wages at West Ham but we're managing to balance the books. Most of the players of my generation came out of football without a penny behind them so if players today have the talent to set themselves up for life, good luck to them. My only grumble, as I outlined in detail earlier, is that managers at the highest level should be equally handsomely rewarded.

I've been in football more than 30 years now, man and boy, player and manager, and I've loved every second. The bad times have been many, but the good times outweigh them. And my proudest boast is that if some disaster happens, if I have a serious falling-out with the board at Upton Park that calls for my departure, I will leave this club in probably the healthiest state it's ever enjoyed. I'll walk out of those doors and think: 'Well Harry, you may be leaving but what a legacy – the finest squad of players at Upton Park in the history of West Ham.' Harry's game isn't all played out yet, believe me. Let's hope the final chapters are as colourful, enjoyable, and damn well bloody exciting as those that have gone before.

Career Statistics

1947 Born 2 March to father Harry and mother Violet in Poplar, East London. Only child.

1963 Chased by all top London clubs but signs schoolboy forms for West Ham after manager Ron Greenwood successfully woos parents.

1963 Wins FA Youth Cup with West Ham. Hammers lose 3–1 at Liverpool in first leg of the final but win a dramatic return 5–2.

1964 Plays for the England team which wins the Junior World Cup in Amsterdam, beating Spain 4–0 in the final.

1965 Makes full West Ham debut on 23 August, the second match of the season, at home to Sunderland. Match finishes 1–1, with Martin Peters heading home Harry's corner for the opening goal.

1966 Scores first goal for Hammers on 8 April in a 4–1 win at Tottenham.

1968 Married at St. Margaret's Church in Barking to Sandra

Harris on 30 June. One of the guests is Hammers team-mate Frank Lampard, later to become Harry's brother-in-law after marrying Sandra's sister Pat.

1970   First son Mark born on 16 April.

1972   Last game for West Ham on 15 April. Hammers lose 2–0 at home to Liverpool to goals from John Toshack and Steve Heighway. Total of 149 League appearances for Hammers with seven goals. Also 26 cup appearances with one goal.

1972   Joins Bournemouth, managed by ex-West Ham team-mate John Bond, for Bournemouth club record of £31,000. First game on 26 August – a 3–2 defeat at Watford.

1973   Second son Jamie born on 25 June.

1974   Joins Norwich, managed by John Bond, on loan but knee injury wrecks permanent move.

1976   Joins Seattle Sounders as player-coach under former Bournemouth team-mate Jimmy Gabriel in the North American Soccer League. Later joined by Bobby Moore and Geoff Hurst.

1977   Reaches the NASL Play-Off Final against New York Cosmos – Pele, Franz Beckenbauer et al. Seattle lose 2–1 to a freak winner.

1979   Leaves Seattle to join Jimmy Gabriel at newly-formed Phoenix Fire. Falls victim to American con-man.

1980   Teams up with old pal Bobby Moore as assistant manager at non-League Oxford City. Travels up from Bournemouth each day for the princely sum of £120 a week.

1981   Invited to become coach at Third Division Bournemouth by manager Dave Webb, the former Chelsea star.

1982   Big comeback as a player in England turns sour. Plays in League Cup tie against Manchester United at Old Trafford in September and scores own goal in defeat.

1982   Takes over as Bournemouth caretaker-manager in

December following the sacking of Dave Webb. First game is at League leaders Lincoln – Bournemouth lose 9–0.

1983 Appointed full-time boss at Dean Court after Webb's replacement Don Megson leaves club in October.

1984 Bournemouth beat Manchester United 2–0 in third round of the FA Cup in January.

1984 Bournemouth win Associate Members Cup in May, beating Hull in the final.

1987 Cherries clinch Third Division championship in May, reaching the dizzy heights of the Second Division (no Premiership then) for the first time. Voted Division Three manager of the year.

1990 Son Jamie makes his professional debut for Bournemouth – a Second Division clash against West Ham.

1990 Bournemouth lose 1–0 at home to Leeds – a defeat which sends them back to Division Three. Match scarred by thousands of Leeds fans going on the rampage at the ground and throughout the town.

1990 Seriously injured in a horrific car accident in Italy during the World Cup. Best friend Brian Tiler tragically killed. Loses sense of smell and taste; fractures skull.

1991 Sells son Jamie to Liverpool in January for an initial fee of £350,000, with a further £350,000 to reach the club based on appearances.

1992 Leaves Bournemouth at end of season following bust-up with the chairman.

1992 Joins West Ham as assistant to manager and big mate Billy Bonds. Hammers have just been relegated from the top flight.

1992 Interviewed by police after gestures to the crowd during a 5–1 win at Bristol City in September.

1993 Hammers beat Cambridge 2–0 in final game of the season in May to clinch promotion back to the top flight.

1994 Takes over from Billy Bonds in controversial circumstances as Hammers manager. Three defeats and two draws in first five League games before a Tony Cottee strike at Aston Villa on 17 September earns first win.

1995 Real danger of relegation as May arrives, with two home games left – against Liverpool and Manchester United. West Ham beat Liverpool 3–0 to guarantee survival. Nothing to play for against United, who must win and hope Blackburn lose at Liverpool to clinch title. Blackburn lose, but Hammers hold United to a draw. West Ham finish 14th, five points clear of relegation slot.

1996 Hammers draw 1–1 at home to Sheffield Wednesday in final match of the season in May to finish in top half (10th) for the first time in 10 years.

1997 West Ham lose 1–0 at home to Second Division Wrexham in the third round of the FA Cup in January. Harry offers resignation. Chairman refuses.

1997 Hammers lose 2–0 at Blackburn in February and relegation seems a certainty.

1997 Signs John Hartson and Paul Kitson later in February and the rest is history. Hammers rally to escape drop and ultimately finish 14th. Hartson and Kitson net 13 League goals between them in last 14 games.

1998 West Ham finish eighth in Premiership, narrowly missing out on a place in Europe.

1998 New season begins in August with West Ham the best-backed outsider with bookies to win the title.

Index